AF479282

Table of contents

	Page
Business Philosophy	6
Gold Bond Days	14
Transition	34
Corporate Staff	36
Hospitality	38
Travel	58
Motivation	72
Sales Promotion	88
Real Estate Investments	92
Family	94
Roots	107
Philanthropy	118
Future	126
Important Dates	134
Awards and Honors	137

__About the Cover:__ Curt Carlson, Chairman of the Board, Carlson Companies, stands in front of the Carlson Companies World Headquarters, Carlson Center, Minnetonka, Minnesota. The $650 million Carlson Center, anchored by the Carlson World Headquarters building, is being developed by Trammell Crow Company, the nation's largest commercial real estate developer. Carlson Center is located about 10 minutes west of downtown Minneapolis.

__Inside cover:__ The dynamic Minneapolis skyline is dominated by the modernistic Hubert H. Humphrey Metrodome, home of baseball's World Series champion Minnesota Twins and football's Minnesota Vikings. Curt Carlson was among eight prominent civic leaders who donated millions of dollars and saved big-league sports for the Twin Cities with the construction of this indoor sports stadium. Carlson also contributed to the vital redevelopment of downtown Minneapolis with his dazzling new flagship Radisson Plaza Hotel and office building (Plaza VII), opened in 1987 on the site of the original Radisson Hotel. The futuristic, $108 million structure is framed by the IDS Center and the Multifoods Tower.

Carlson Companies Board of Directors includes (standing from left): Rodney M. Wilson, banker Carl R. Pohlad, Marilyn C. Nelson, and attorney Matthew J. Levitt. Seated are Barbara C. Gage and Curtis L. Carlson, company founder and board chairman of his company which is celebrating 50 years.

This book is dedicated to all those who made the magnificent journey from a 16th century farm-house on the soil of Sweden, to those who are working daily to build Carlson's World and to those who are keeping the dream alive as we pre-pare for the 21st century.

Curt Carlson

The Ultra Entrepreneur

Sky-high in the Carlson Companies jetcraft, Curt Carlson and his wife, Arleen, relax en route to another business destination. Carlson, an entrepreneurial pioneer and owner of one of America's largest privately held corporations, is founder and chairman of the board of a multi-billion-dollar group of service companies operating in the primary businesses of marketing/motivation, travel, hospitality, sales promotion and real estate investments. Arleen, his college sweetheart and wife of fifty years, is constant companion, partner, mother of their two daughters, grandmother to seven and "First Lady" of the Carlson family of companies. In 1988, Carlson marks 50 years of successful business.

The Ultra Entrepreneur

Curt Carlson

PRODUCER KARL W. GULLERS   TEXT WILLMON L. WHITE   GULLERS PICTORIAL INC.

*As a Swedish-American success story, Curt Carlson and his wife, Arleen,
enjoy a personal relationship with Carl XVI Gustaf, King of Sweden.*

Two self-made men, Curt Carlson and U.S. President Ronald Reagan, share many common beliefs: patriotism, free enterprise, the importance of traditional values such as hard work, family loyalty and religious faith.

Business Philosophy

Board chairman and sole owner of Carlson Companies, Curtis LeRoy Carlson represents a classic rags-to-riches success story. He heads an international business conglomerate including more than 75 companies employing some 50,000 people. Carlson Companies is one of America's largest privately-held firms.

Chairman of the Board

The philosophy which governs my actions and decisions in the business world has been shaped by my experience as an entrepreneur. It is comprised of definite guidelines which I feel are necessary for corporate success. These guidelines are a result of my experience in the day-to-day process of business rather than a conscious effort to define specific rules of success.

Fundamental to my business philosophy is a firm belief in the free enterprise system. To thrive effectively within this system, a successful business must produce a profit. Accordingly, I consider profit to be an honorable and essential ingredient of the free enterprise system.

A profitable company contributes immeasurably to the social, cultural and economic growth of a community and a nation by providing jobs, good salaries, plus opportunities for advancement and education. All these factors are essential for the self-respect of employees and for their dignity, particularly in the eyes of their families and of society at large.

Conversely, the company which operates with limited or no profit is a parasite which gnaws away at the free enterprise system, preying upon the welfare of the individuals by causing low salaries, reduced opportunities for advancement, few employee fringe benefits, and possible loss of jobs. These conditions tend to generate unrest and discontent in society along with feelings of bitterness toward business.

The tempo of change is increasing at a rapid pace. Every change in the state-of-the-art of enterprise and the usual conduct of our economy presents an opportunity to fulfill new needs. By answering needs effectively, one develops the potential of a profitable business. To grow, a company must develop a fountainhead of capital which can generate the necessary funds to assure expansion and permit diversification. When this fountainhead is firmly established, soundly managed, and tightly controlled, a company can further guarantee its success through diversification by expanding into varied fields.

Through diversification, a businessman reduces the risk of capital losses. Diversification then becomes a tremendous tool for continued success.

Diversification, however, carries with it basic risks because, with each new endeavor, the possibility of failure looms on the horizon. This is a great concern for any company president; personally, I find the most difficult part of my job is the mental stress about the great risks we take in expansion and diversification.

Yet, I firmly believe that there is no place in the business world for the status quo—remaining constant or standing still—since there are always others moving rapidly behind who will accelerate quickly and pass you by if your momentum is reduced. I have always maintained that you will stay even with your competitor by working five days a week, but you can get ahead of your competition by working six days. The old saying is still true: "The harder I work, the luckier I get."

A successful business should always be ready for change and maintain enough flexibility to move quickly and adapt readily to fluctuating economic conditions.

To produce a good product or service and generate the momentum necessary for success, a business must have the support and enthusiasm of its employees. The officers of a company can set priorities and chart the course of business, but the employees must carry out the programs and ideas to make them work. The management of a company can build an organization, but it is the organization—the people—which builds the company. Therefore, employees are the most important asset of a business. The employees make the company move forward; and, without their loyalty and dedication, the best business programs and ideas in the world are worthless.

The task of commanding employee loyalty and dedication is a difficult one that requires the company to create a stimulating business climate and provide meaningful motivation for its employees. I have learned that the best means of motivating is the proper use of goals—specific, measurable, reasonable goals—that are tied to a definite timeframe. They must be simple enough so that both the supervisors and the employee understand them clearly. A monthly published list of the current standing against the quota is a must. The reward for achievement must be worthwhile and commensurate with the quota.

The employee with a clearly defined career goal makes a positive contribution to the company by directing his or her daily actions toward this specific objective. When I started in business some fifty years ago, I wrote the next goal that I hoped to attain on a piece of paper, folded it carefully, and carried it in my billfold. When I reached that goal, I removed the piece of paper and threw it away. But I set a new goal and wrote it on another piece of paper and carried it with me until that goal was reached. As our organization grew, my personal goals were transferred into company objectives.

Originally, we set our sights on doubling our revenues every four years. Obviously, we gained some measure of success, as we have achieved an average sales increase of 33 percent compounded stretching over more than four decades. Our capitalization base has mushroomed to such an extent that now we look only for a 15 percent annual increase, which results in doubling our revenues every five years.

Setting any goal is meaningless unless your earnings plus your borrowing capacity is at a level that can be financed. Adding more stores, more sales personnel and more inventory costs money. This must be provided for in a strategic analysis before setting your goal.

*I*n addition to establishing proper goals, a successful company must create and maintain a climate of creativity and imagination among its employees if it is to recognize and properly satisfy consumer needs. Innovations that add value greater than your competition are essential to continued growth and marketing breakthroughs.

An imaginative company is one that can recognize a public need, properly analyze that need, develop the ideas which meet that need and then carry these ideas to their successful fruition.

A creative company must have the foresight to see all the manifold aspects of a consumer problem and work, with an attitude of service-effectiveness, toward the long-range profit goal rather than the near-term advantage of quick profit.

To attain the long-range view necessary for stable and steady growth, a company depends heavily on its executives and key employees for the in-depth thought that goes into business planning and the attainment of the company's mission. An imaginative and creative executive who has a history of job stability and is deeply involved in his responsibility will instill those same qualities in the employees who work for him. Together they will spark the company to move forward in meaningful and forceful directions that will capture the attention of the consumer.

Operating a successful business such as Carlson Companies is in many respects similar to running a successful political campaign, except that a businessman does not have as much time to prove a program viable as does the politician. In the world of business, the public votes with its dollars and, in today's increasingly international marketplace, with its yen, its marks, its pesos, its lire. Only as long as a company can produce a desired, worthwhile and needed product or service, and can command public respect, will it receive the public currency and succeed.

While I believe firmly in goals and in employee motivation to meet specified goals, I believe with equal conviction that a businessman or woman must never be content with having reached a goal. **I consider a goal as a milestone marker on a journey rather than a final destination.** Along the route, new opportunities develop, new directions become apparent and new and exciting goals can be set—and met.

Carlson Companies is not satisfied to be one of the largest privately-owned and diversified international corporations. Our entire executive group has visions of greatness and that vision runs deep within the rank and file of our company.

*M*y business credo holds that action should triumph over analysis. My company presidents and top staff people are "biased" toward action; and they are proud of the progress our company is chalking up because they are an integral part of the decision-making process. People work for more than money, and there's **esprit de corps** that goes beyond the paycheck. It's the desire and determination to achieve, to grow in their careers and the excitement of the quest for excellence.

Times, markets, methods and customers change. But within Carlson Companies, the entrepreneurial spirit still thrives.

President of the Company

Much of my business philosophy is deeply intertwined with my relationship with Curt Carlson for 20 years, and employing this philosophy within the four operating groups of Carlson Companies. Because of my marketing background, I would probably place slightly more emphasis on market-related strategies than Curt, but in essence many of my personal business philosophies closely mirror his.

I believe in the entrepreneurial approach to running businesses and profit centers. This means that as much as possible within appropriate fiscal restraints we want a company CEO and his management team to run a company as if it were his own business. Large operations must be broken down into profit centers so that the parent corporation can measure the success of individual managers. Similarly, the management team and the employee groups can also see their own impact on the results of their operation.

I believe in focusing on businesses where we have experience, a synergistic advantage and market leadership. A company is simply an organization of individuals. It can only do so many tasks well. With no limits on the scope of your activity, you obviously can't keep up with competition.

I believe that business decisions must be made within the context of long-term market share leadership and balanced by short-term cash flow and return-on-investment needs of the operating company. The goal of Carlson Companies is to be Number One in every market segment where we operate. Historically in most businesses the market share leader achieves the highest level of earnings among the competitors in that universe.

In service businesses, management and your employees are the major key to success. Capital is important, of course, but goals cannot be achieved without the people who come up with the ideas to harness capital and turn those goals into products and services that customers want. Related to this, a company must have growth

Edwin C. "Skip" Gage, 20 years with Carlson Companies, is president and chief operating officer. He brings to the corporation a spirit of competition that made him a tennis star at Northwestern University.

and continued opportunity to motivate its employees to stretch for excellence and high achievement.

We always take a customer-driven attitude. Thus, it is profoundly important that an organization understands what the customer needs and wants so that goods and services can be sold. Management must constantly strive to stay in tune with customers because these needs and wants are in a constant state of change.

Quality is exceedingly important when defining a service product. Quality is a relative term based on the other products and services offered in the specific market universe. When price is equal, the customer's best value is created by quality difference. Quality is often real as well as perceived. Creating a positive perception of quality is a vital factor in salesmanship.

My basic business philosophy is grounded in the belief that a business makes a substantial contribution to society through the creation of goods, services and the providing of jobs to our valued employees. It is therefore essential that a business make an adequate return on investment so that it can survive and continue to make its contribution to society.

Carlson Companies
WORLD HEADQ

Founder Curt Carlson (left) before the world headquarters that served Gold Bond Stamp Company and Carlson Companies, Inc. since it opened in 1962. In 1989, most of the operation will move to the new Carlson Center being built west of Minneapolis. The flags represent some of the 34 nations where Carlson Companies does business.

Curt Carlson travels the world in managing and expanding his international business empire—and sometimes by exotic modes of transportation. Carlson Travel Group itself is the largest travel operation in North America, with more than 600 outlets serving the markets of commercial, leisure and incentive travel.

Harry Greenough has been Curt Carlson's close friend, confidant, and right-hand man for over 30 years. The No. 2 salesman after Curt himself, Greenough helped to motivate sales people to meet their quotas and chalk up success in the company's five-year plans. Once president of Gold Bond Stamp Company, Greenough recently retired as a Carlson Companies vice president and vice chairman of Carlson Marketing Group.

	1978		1979		1980		1981		19
	PLAN	ACTUAL	PLAN	ACTUAL	PLAN	ACTUAL	PLAN	ACTUAL	PLA
TING	200	**249**	251	**313**	500		347		356
	90	**90**	105	**110**			140		
	20	**30**	23						
RACT	8	**11**	10	**18**			14		
	163	**164**	175				205		
OM	150	**216**	230				350		
	10		60				71		

Ann Richardson is a case study in what a Carlson employee can accomplish who works hard, takes pride in loyalty and measures up to the Carlson system of goal-setting and achievement. Ms. Richardson has been with the company more than 30 years, starting as a secretary. Today, she is vice president of administration for Carlson Companies and president of CSA, Inc., the company's construction and design arm.

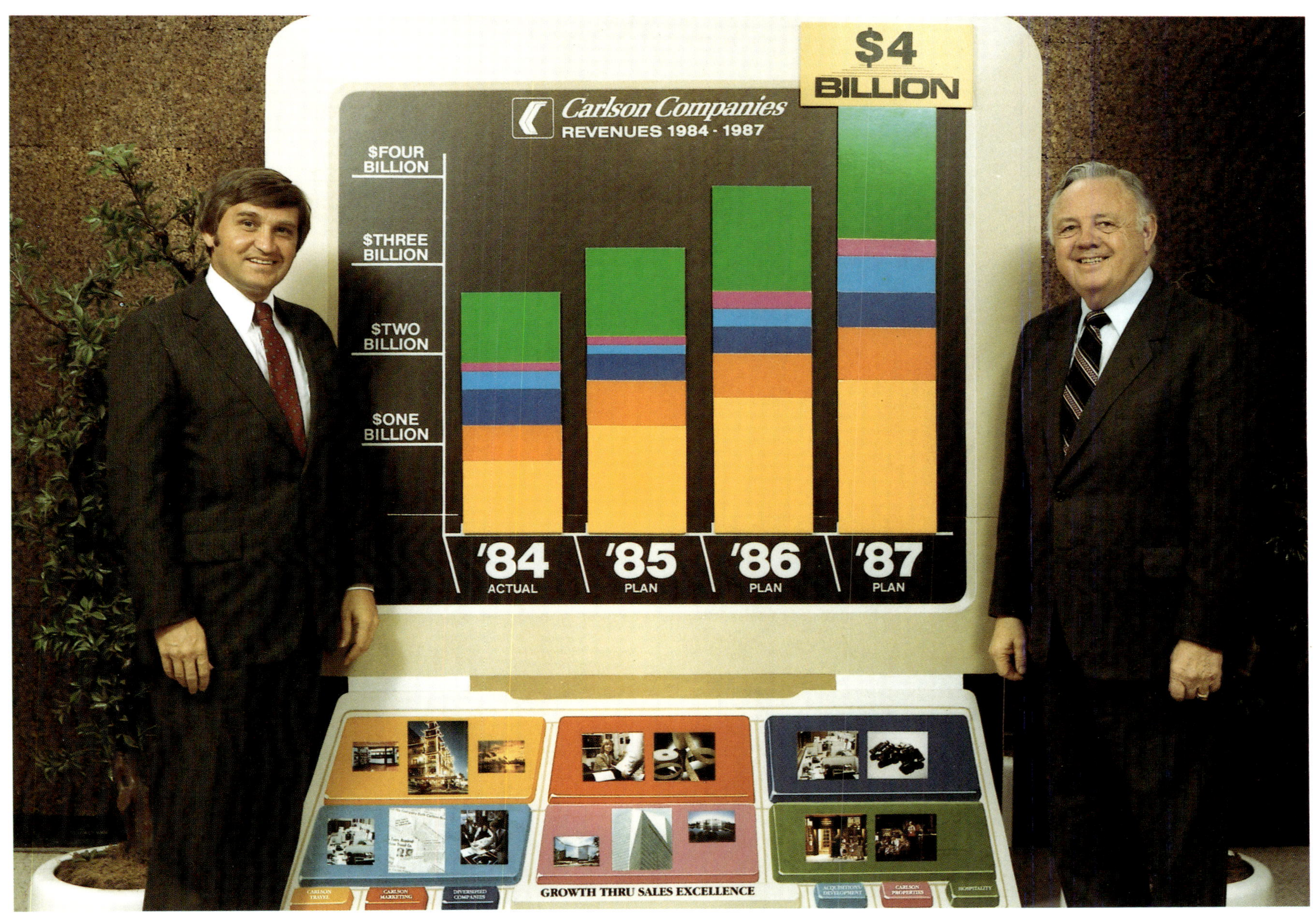

Carlson Companies, with a slogan of "Growth Thru Sales Excellence," completed a five-year growth plan to achieve annual revenues of $4 billion in 1987. Edwin C. "Skip" Gage, president and chief operating officer, leads a goal-driven management team which strives to carry on Curt Carlson's entrepreneurial spirit. In 1988, Carlson celebrates his 50th year in business. Now. . .turn the page to see how it all began.

Gold Bond Days

Nobody knows whether entrepreneurs are made or born, but they all seem to share some character traits, personality profiles and behavioral patterns. Those who have studied the breed — both business analysts and psychologists — have found that entrepreneurs take total responsibility for their own motivation. They skate on the edge of recklessness in taking risks; it is almost as if they cannot imagine failure. They are obsessed with personal achievement and seem to possess special skill in setting and meeting specific goals. They are willing to invest huge amounts of time and effort and make personal sacrifices, because their work is exhilarating. Most of all, entrepreneurs believe they are *special and invincible.*

Such a man is Curtis LeRoy Carlson, one of America's classic entrepreneurs. With Gold Bond trading stamps, he was practicing and perfecting his own brand of free-wheeling free enterprise five decades before the term "entrepreneur" came into current vogue. The Minnesota-based near-billionaire is, in fact, the *ultra* entrepreneur. He has harnessed his fearless, highly-focused instincts and parlayed them not merely into a spectacu-

Minneapolis during the boyhood years of Curt Carlson had already developed from a frontier lumber town to a thriving metropolitan magnet of the Upper Midwest. Like thousands of Scandinavian immigrants, Carlson's father was drawn from the farm to the city's bustling industry, commerce and aura of opportunity. Here, Curt would ride streetcars to golf caddy, hustle newspapers, help in his father's grocery, work his way through college and, borrowing $50, launch Gold Bond trading stamps, parent of today's multi-billion-dollar empire.

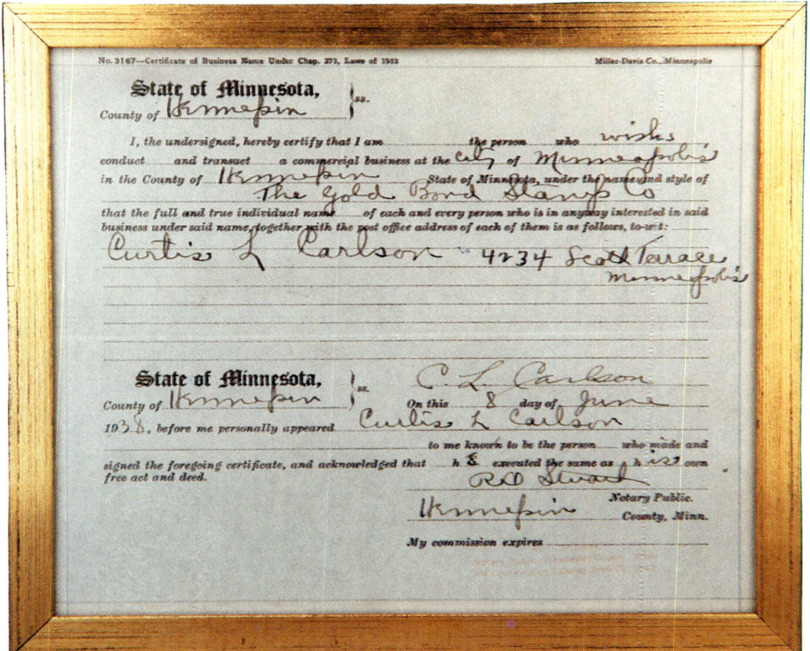

Gold Bond Stamp Co. was chartered on June 8, 1938, with this document in State of Minnesota, County of Hennepin.

Curt Carlson (second from right) worked his way through college during Depression days, driving a "soda pop" beverage truck. Curt's older brother, Ken, is pictured at far left in the 1930s.

Carlson as a sophomore at the University of Minnesota. This natty tweed suit caught the eye of classmate Arleen Martin; they were married in 1938, the year Gold Bond was created.

The original Gold Bond trading stamp. This gummed piece of paper launched a business which today includes 75 corporations and employs more than 50,000 men and women.

larly successful business enterprise, but rather into an ever-expanding universe of companies which comprises one of the nation's largest private empires. Increasingly, it stretches around the globe.

Carlson has directed the pure, powerful laser-beam of the entrepreneurial spirit through the polished prism of his own personal goals and synergistic style. The result: the release of new energy to create dozens of international corporations operating in a broad spectrum of industries. Few entrepreneurs in the second half of the 20th century have been so effective in reaching beyond merely outstanding achievement to a level of mega-success.

Curt Carlson transplanted the trading stamp concept from department stores to small grocery stores and other neighborhood merchants. As a star salesman for Procter & Gamble, he reasoned that incentives would help independent grocers compete with larger markets. Early to sign up were Bistodeau Brothers of Minneapolis (top); Carlson installed the homemade signs himself. Carlson's big breakthrough came in the early 1950s when he convinced the Super Valu supermarket chain (see below) to take on Gold Bond trading stamps. A new era was unfolding.

The story begins with Carlson's father, Charles, a Swedish immigrant who left a Minnesota farm at age 19 for Minneapolis (see "Roots," page 107). The young man took a job driving a sprinkler wagon, wetting down dusty streets in Minneapolis. In 1905 he married Letha Peterson and after the birth in 1914 of Curtis — the third of five children — the father found a better job with a wholesale grocery firm. He called on small neighborhood grocers in Minneapolis, working 14-hour days. It was a family ritual, however, that the evening meal waited until father arrived home from work, usually about 8 or 8:30 p.m.

Letha Carlson was a strong and loving mother, the family's cornerstone and vital force. She was the primary advocate of the Carlson family credo: "Work hard. Ask for no hand-outs. Be dependable. Manage your money. And never give up." Ambitious herself and seeming to thrive on work, she did housekeeping for a Methodist clergyman when she was 16 years old, after her marriage opened a bakery to help support her young family and still had time to be active in her church.

"She ran the family," says Carlson today, "and we all knew it. Other mothers might warn kids that if they misbehaved, father would deal with them harshly. In our house, it was the reverse. I remember once when I was a golf caddy, probably no more than 11 years old. On Saturdays, I rode the streetcar to the country club where I made 75 cents a round. I was tired one morning and just stood there and let the streetcar pass. Mom, who was watching from the window, was out there like a shot. She told me in unmistakable terms that my puny excuse of just being tired' was unacceptable. I was to be on the next streetcar or walk to the golf course if necessary to do my job carrying those golf bags."

Curt's father eventually opened up his own neighborhood grocery store after he left the wholesale food business. As a young boy, Curt earned money after school by working in the store. Here he received his first taste of food retailing that would play a significant role in the creation of the Gold Bond Trading Stamp Company and other entrepreneurial ventures.

"My father was a good, hardworking salesman," says Carlson. "Although he didn't leave me a large estate, he left me something more valuable. He told me, 'Curt, I'm going to give you

Saturday was the big sales day at grocery stores, but Gold Bond introduced the idea of a "Second Saturday" by offering double trading stamps on Wednesdays. "If it doesn't work," Carlson told cautious clients, "it will cost you nothing." As Gold Bond expanded, the entrepreneur needed $1,000 for signs, stamps and saver books. A prominent Minneapolis banker said "no" to protect Curt from what he thought would be sure failure. Right: Seizing every chance to promote Gold Bond, Curt appears in a newspaper photo heralding spring planting. He had just signed up a prominent seed company to give stamps with seeds.

the whole United States as your territory'." As later developments showed, Curt successfully sold that territory, and then some — going international.

Growing up street-smart in hard times, Curt was 10 years old when he took his first job as a golf caddy. At age 11, he earned his first newspaper route when the circulation manager challenged him to sell more new subscriptions than the incumbent route carrier.

During the next few years, young Curt operated as many as three newspaper routes at one time, subcontracting two of them to his brothers and realizing a small profit on each one. He still supervised these routes after he graduated from high school and entered the University of Minnesota.

He also operated a corner newsstand at a busy streetcar intersection where he sold newspapers. His biggest sales day was on "Black Tuesday," October 29, 1929. The stock market crash signaled the onset of the Great Depression. Carlson, at age 15, together with Americans everywhere, faced a future fraught with uncertainty.

"Times *were* tough those depression days," says Carlson today, "but any kid who wanted to work and would go after it could make a buck or two. Lawns still had to be mowed, snow shoveled, fences painted and groceries delivered. Our family never had much money but I don't remember feeling poor. Everybody was in the same boat. There's always hope and opportunity in every bleak situation. Remember the story of the kid who found himself waist deep in horse manure? He was such an optimist that he started shoveling himself out. 'With all this stuff,' he said, 'there must be a pony in here somewhere'."

One of Curt's early "ponies" was a blue Chevrolet convertible — an awesome status symbol for a high school youngster in the depths of the depression. To get the car he worked — in addition to his newspaper routes and as a golf caddy — as a page at the Farmers and Mechanics Savings Bank in Minneapolis.

If this sounds like Horatio Alger, there's good reason. Horatio Alger, Jr. was a real Boston boy who survived severe childhood illness and slow development in walking and talking. But he went on to enter Harvard at 16, graduate into the clergy, travel in Europe and to write 125 books and create 135 heroes and heroines. If he had lived in the last half of the 19th century, Curt Carlson — with his own story of "pluck, perseverance and manly independence" — might have been one of those young heroes. It's fitting that Carlson received the national Horatio Alger Award in 1978 from the Horatio Alger Association of Distinguished Americans.

It wasn't the Horatio Alger stories that inspired Curt Carlson, however, but rather a famous lecture called "Acres of Diamonds." The author was Russell Herman Conwell, a Union soldier, Baptist preacher, founder of Philadelphia's Temple University and an entrepreneur. In the lecture — given more than 6,000 times over a 40-year span and earning $8 million — Conwell told of a man who roamed the world in search of fame and fortune and who died, never discovering a diamond mine in his own backyard.

Curt Carlson began to discover his own "acre of diamonds" and an instinctive flair for salesmanship about the time he graduated from Minneapolis' West High School in 1932. He had been president of his Hi-Y (YMCA) club in high school and was rushing chairman and president of his college fraternity, Sigma Phi Epsilon. Especially persuasive in recruiting new members, he had found his calling.

"Mom wanted me to go into law," says Curt. "But deep in my heart I loved selling and influencing people. One of the most comforting and soothing sounds in the world is the voice of a master salesman when he really goes to work. Selling isn't just moving merchandise. It requires an ability to get people to see your point of view. And no sale is a good sale unless it's a 'win-win' situation for both salesman and customer. I'm well aware that salesmen rank with politicians as the least-admired professionals. But a good salesman *earns* respect. Remember," says Carlson, "if somebody didn't sell it, the whole economy would slow to a walk and unemployment would skyrocket."

Working his way through college, Carlson drove a "soda pop" delivery truck and sold advertising. He graduated from the University of Minnesota with an economics degree in 1937. His grades had improved markedly after meeting an attractive green-eyed blonde, Arleen Martin, in a political science class. Carlson remembers the moment with a twinkle in his eye.

"I sat down next to her, leaned over, cupped my hand to her ear and whispered. 'I've been going to this school over three years and you're exactly the girl I've been looking for'." He walked her to her next class, hung his fraternity pin on her before the year was out and became officially engaged in his senior year. Curt and Arleen were married one year later and their first child, Marilyn, was born a year after that.

On graduation, the Carnation Company offered Carlson an "Internship for Fulltime Executives," a promising job with a bright future and starting pay of $125 a month, among the highest offered to graduates. But Curt took another offer from Procter & Gamble for $110 monthly in order to stay in Minneapolis near his fiancee. Soon he was hawking soap and shortening to grocers in the neighborhoods where he had grown up. It was "sales wars" on the retail battlefield, pushing Oxydol, Camay, Ivory Flakes, Dreft and Crisco against the competing brandnames of Colgate and Lever Brothers. Curt learned the battle plan well: "Put in more hours. Make more calls. Show them your product is better. Demand prime shelf space and *get up* those displays." P&G's tough Midwest district manager, C.W. Mussett, told Curt: "Be aggressive. If you don't get thrown out of at least one grocery store a week, you're not selling hard enough."

At age 23, sales ace Carlson was showing the largest percentage increase in district sales over the previous year. His reward was an engraved gold watch and a $330 bonus. Curt was proud, but behind that pride was the nagging thought of the money he would have earned if he had been selling soap for himself. As an entrepreneur, Curt Carlson was ready to hatch and build his own nest egg.

Psychologists who have studied invention and innovation say there is, more often than not, a magic moment when the idea sparks. The old cartoon of the light bulb over the head illustrates that moment almost literally. With great clarity, the brain "sees" how to solve the problem, knows the answer to the big question, realizes the pure potential of an opportunity and how to harness it for advancement.

For Curt Carlson, the moment came one day when he ran across a yellowed, half-filled S&H trading stamp book at the home of the Martins, his in-laws. The saver book reminded him of Leader's department store in Minneapolis which gave one Red Security Stamp for each ten cents of purchase. When you filled a book, you redeemed it for $2 cash. Trading stamps were nothing new; they had been in use for decades by some department stores.

But the light bulb in Carlson's head lit another pathway. Why not, Curt reasoned, sell trading stamps to grocery stores to offer their customers as incentives. Stamps made even more sense for grocers than department stores because food markets sold essentially the same products. The only reason to shop one store over another was price, service perhaps, and some added incentive — such as little gummed pieces of paper that housewives might save in books and redeem for cash or merchandise. Carlson understood the retail food business — he had worked long hours in it with his father, and he had successfully sold soap and shortening to grocers. The logic came like a thunderbolt: *Why not trading stamps?* With the promotional skills he'd learned with P&G, Curt felt confident he could convince small grocers that stamps would stimulate business.

Carlson discussed his scheme with anybody who would listen — friends, family, former professors and bankers. Virtually everyone — except Arleen's father, Charles Martin — told Curt it was too risky. The naysayers reminded Carlson he had a good job with Procter & Gamble, that Arleen was pregnant and the waves of economic depression still washed across the nation. "Don't do it. Don't do it *now!*" was the almost unanimous advice of his elder advisors.

But the true entrepreneur listens to little but his inner voice; Carlson's instincts told him *"Do* it. Do it *now!"* On June 8, 1938, Curt registered Gold Bond Stamp Company — gold for value, bond for safety — with the State of Minnesota in Hennepin County.

He then proceeded to choose a design for his stamps (5,000 to a pad), print stamp saver books and prepare contract agreements for his future customers. Carlson continued to work for P&G during the day. But in the evenings and on weekends he persuaded small neighborhood grocers to try trading stamps. Their decision came hard, for the depression had seriously eroded the small retailer's income, and giving up another two percent of the gross sales for Gold Bond stamps seemed risky. Many shook their heads and said no.

Gold Bond's office was a desk and a mail drop in Minneapolis' Plymouth Building at a cost of $30 per month, utilities included. Someone else's secretary answered his phone for $5 a month. There were few calls, but then came a breakthrough.

The Grant Brothers grocery on 25th Street in south Minneapolis was the first to sign up. That first stamp order totaled $14.50 and gave "Grant" the exclusive right to distribute Gold Bond stamps for a 25-block area. For the grand opening, Carlson hung homemade signs on the outside and wire-strung banners and balloons inside. The night before, Curt took Arleen down to the store and, by flashlight, proudly showed off his customer. "If it works," he told her, "there are thousands of stores like this all over America that will buy and use Gold Bond stamps." Arleen smiled and hoped so.

By the end of 1938, Gold Bond had developed 40 grocery accounts and Carlson was still a leading salesman for Procter & Gamble. He was making $150 a month plus bonuses but he knew it was time to cut the umbilical cord. Entrepreneurs cannot tolerate three things: corporate red tape, having other people tell them what to do, and making other people rich. He left P&G with no regrets, an outstanding sales record and an offer to return if Gold Bond failed.

December 7, 1941 — "a day that shall live in infamy." The Japanese attacked Pearl Harbor and the U.S. Congress immediately instituted the military draft and prepared for war. Carlson was classified 1-A and instructed to be ready for call-up for duty at any time.

From among his salesmen, Curt chose Truman Johnson to be his successor. Johnson was headquartered in Green Bay with eastern Wisconsin as his Gold Bond territory. Although not the top salesman of the group and considerably older than Carlson, he had other qualities that made him first choice. Johnson was a top-notch administrator and an excellent sales manager — most important because Gold Bond was sales-driven. Another valuable characteristic was his mindset on profitability. Salesmen who didn't pay their own way by meeting ambitious goals were quickly replaced.

Carlson's extended negotiations with Johnson came to a conclusion when Curt received a letter from the U.S. Department of Defense advising him to tidy up his affairs and be prepared to report in 90 days. Instead of a hired president for Gold Bond, Carlson took a partner. He sold 49 percent to Johnson and retained 49 percent. One percent each went to Joe Hunt, Carlson's most loyal employee, and Dick Evenson, a friend of both Curt and Truman Johnson.

"I was now ready to go," recalls Carlson. "Joe Hunt had already been called up and we arranged to continue to send his full salary each month to his wife. My wife, Arleen, was to receive half of the profit. Everything else remained in place. In the meantime, my second daughter, Barbara, was born. As fate would have it, I shortly received another notice that, as the father of two children, I was now reclassified and would only be called up in a national emergency."

Carlson took back the title of Gold Bond president and chief executive officer and Truman Johnson assumed the title of chairman. At the end of 1941, Gold Bond had 400 clients in Minnesota, Wisconsin and Iowa, but the onset of World War II destroyed two-thirds of the business. What with scarcities and rationing, grocers and service stations did not need trading stamps to draw customers.

After the war, Gold Bond was off and running again as trading stamp fever swept the nation. Carlson hired new salesmen to solidify his position in the Midwest and open new territory in Indiana, Texas, Oregon and other states. Curt Carlson didn't invent the trading stamps but he made marketing history by showing how far a good idea could be carried. Gas stations and dry cleaners began to offer stamps and one crackerjack salesman named Vernon McCoy sold stamps to movie theaters, feed and grain stores, even undertakers and a turkey hatchery. American housewives were having a love affair with the trading stamp and its tangible rewards.

As always, Carlson's main strength was his concentration on goals. As a soap salesman he carried his personal goals on a slip of paper in his wallet — the first was to make $100 a week plus salary. When that goal was reached, he wrote down another and placed it behind his driver's license. His first goals were for only one year. By 1942, he was sufficiently knowledgeable about the potential of his business to set five-year goals.

"To succeed you must eat, sleep and dream your goals and quotas," says Carlson. "When you're brushing your teeth, when you're driving to work, when you're out relaxing on the boat, your mind will be searching for ways and means to achieve your goal. It's a fact, an *absolute* fact: You will never make as much progress without targets as you will with goal setting.''

In 1946 Carlson and partner Johnson mapped a new five-year growth plan to expand Gold Bond into seven states and they set a profit goal of $200,000. Curt incorporated the goal into a slogan — "It Shall Be Done in '51" — the first of many targets hit and surpassed. His formula for success is deceptively simple: $G+I+P=S^n$ — Goals plus *Inspiration* plus *Perspiration* equals *Success* to the *nth power*.

Gold Bond was doing well selling independent retailers and by 1951 was operating in 11 states and making a national impact. But Carlson's burning ambition was to vault into the big time by capturing a major grocery chain. The big breakthrough came in 1953 when both Red Owl stores and Super Valu (the nation's largest food retailing chain) finally began to listen. Red Owl wanted Gold Bond to cut the value of each trading stamp in half by requiring consumers to save twice as many stamps to earn a particular premium. This, of course, would reduce Red Owl's cost of offering stamps by one-half. Curt considered the proposal, but refused, knowing that his larger arch rival, S&H Green Stamps, would be offering a better stamp program to their customers.

Three days later, Super Valu called Carlson to say their 20-member retail advisory committee would vote on whether to sign on with Gold Bond. Not all members of this chain of independent grocers favored trading stamps. Carlson recalls sitting outside the meeting room, sweating blood. Inside, angry voices and table fist-pounding could be heard. "But they voted 11 to 9 in favor of our plan," says Curt, "and not a store dropped from the Super Valu chain. Gold Bond proved to be the promotional phenomenon of the entire food retailing industry. The whole grocery world was in an uproar!"

Super Valu's sales jumped 60 percent during the first 10 months it offered Gold Bond stamps. Grocery executives from several states beat a path to Minneapolis to investigate this tiny stamp with such an unbelievable appeal to housewives. Soon Carlson was introducing Gold Bond into supermarkets across the nation. Other trading stamp companies joined the grocery chain bonanza and new stamp companies spread like wildfire. Carlson himself created a spin-off stamp company for the Kroger grocery chain and later sold it for $1 million.

The stamp frenzy continued unabated through the 1950s and 1960s. The trading stamp catalog, it seemed, had replaced the Sears and Roebuck catalog as the American family's favorite "wish book." At its peak, Gold Bond operated 330 redemption centers, "stores" where stampsavers exchanged their filled books for merchandise. The trading stamp business skyrocketed from 23 billion stamps in 1952 — $50 million in business — to 20 times that amount in 1968. Gold Bond grabbed a major share of the billion-dollar industry.

During the building years of the Gold Bond organization, Curt's three brothers played important roles. Ken, the oldest, helped Carlson enter the real estate business by opening 330 Gold Bond redemption centers and seven premium warehouses. He kept track of the purchasing and installation of fixtures in these facilities, was responsible for lease renewals and, in some cases, bought the real estate. Dean and Warren Carlson, Curt's two younger brothers, both worked their way up from salesmen to vice presidents and regional managers of Gold Bond. All three brothers are now retired. Sister Aileen's husband, Dwight Miller, also had a place in the history of Gold Bond's growth; he was the official photographer for many years at the company's semi-annual meetings and was always on hand to take pictures of winners during various award ceremonies.

In 1957, Carlson had bought out Truman Johnson, his partner for 14 years. It was the last time the Minnesota entrepreneur would give up controlling stock of his business and share leadership with anyone. "I felt strongly about keeping Carlson Companies private," he says today. "Having two CEOs of equal power simply doesn't work in our competitive economy. It never has and it never will. Two bosses may temporarily cooperate when the company is struggling but not for long. Sooner or later, egos get in the way of effective management."

Carlson adds: "A substantial number of variables tend to split objectives and fragment the mission. This confuses the troops and encourages individuals to break rank and march in different directions. Internal maneuvers and 'politicking' are seldom in favor of the company's greatest good. Instead, the company's objectives are determined by each individual, based on his own benefit."

In Gold Bond, the substantial difference in the age and personal ambition of the two partners created major barriers to moving the company forward. Carlson wanted to build Gold Bond for greater revenues, profits and long-term growth. Johnson wanted to maximize profits short-term in contemplation of a possible sellout — and favored declaring maximum dividends rather than continuing the practice of reinvesting all earnings into growth capital.

"An entrepreneur," Carlson states with conviction, "simply must be free to pursue his own vision. He cannot be confused or confuse his company team by accepting compromises necessary to please another equity partner. He must have full managerial power to press toward goals *he alone* feels are most important. He needs the ability to move decisively and avoid the bureaucratic quicksand of publicly-held corporations. The lone entrepreneur has no worry about takeover attempts. Finally," Curt says with the experience of a highly visible man who can appreciate it, "he enjoys precious privacy."

By the mid-1960s, Carlson had exported Gold Bond trading stamps into Canada, the Caribbean, Japan and England. But he realized that the U.S. market was super-saturated and the handwriting on the wall read: "No promotional scheme reaps huge profits forever — not even trading stamps." For the first time, Curt came face to face with the fact he couldn't achieve that year's goal, even on paper. At the time, 19 of the 20 largest supermarket chains carried some form of incentive stamps and so did 50 percent of the nation's petroleum service stations. Clearly, the time had come to diversify in America and to expand Gold Bond overseas.

Trading stamps are not dead, and Carlson believes they will re-emerge in the U.S. marketplace in a new dress, including exciting innovations, as a time-tested consumer motivation tool to help thousands of businesses to increase sales and market share.

In Japan, meanwhile, trading stamps have captured and held the imagination of the Asian consumer. Back in 1968, Carlson Companies entered into a joint-venture relationship with Mitsubishi, the Japanese industrial giant. Gold Bond had operated independently there for three years but was required by law to take a Japanese partner. The offspring was Gold Bond Japan Ltd., the main business of which was to promote and market trading stamps under the trade names of Gold Star and Gift Bond. "Stamp fever" infected the Japanese just as it did Americans in earlier years. After Mitsubishi adopted Gold Star trad-

Fountain Grill

SNYDER BRO'S

SNYDER BROS SAVE

MIDWAY CUT RATE DRUGS

Snyder Bros Drugs

LOWEST PRICES ALWAYS

FILL PRESCRIPTIONS
SERVICE • ACCURATELY FILLED

Snyder Bros.

WE GIVE GOLD BOND STAMPS

SAVE at our BIG January SOAP SALE

Save GOLD BOND STAMPS

MONEY BACK FOR MONEY SPENT BY SAVING GOLD BOND STAMPS

SUPER VALUE Days SAVE NOW!

Save! SUPER VALUE DAYS!

Year's Biggest Sale NOW ON

GOLD BOND STAMPS

ing stamps for hundreds of their grocery outlets, customers swarmed to earn them with purchases.

Today, Gold Bond Japan has expanded into Kentucky Fried Chicken operations throughout the oriental nation. The promising partnership between Carlson Companies and Mitsubishi has resulted in the strategic study of several other joint business ventures which may make future business-page headlines. Among them are marketing, promotion, and restaurant enterprises similar to those which Carlson Companies developed in the United States, Canada and Europe.

Gold Bond trading stamps, created in 1938, was the foundation, the fountainhead, to the Carlson Companies' diverse international empire. This heritage lives on today both in traditional Gold Bond stamp programs and in related new market-incentive concepts and promotional pioneering.

The entrepreneurial spark lit by 24-year-old Curtis Carlson a half century ago burns brightly in the galaxy of companies he has created and acquired. As charismatic Curt, now 74, puts it: "You can't play it safe and be an entrepreneur. You take risks. You just jump in. If things turn out wrong, then you make them right and take another run at it. If you have the management capability and the iron stomach for exchanging reward potential for security, the quickest road to success and riches is through entrepreneurship."

Drug stores and other merchants joined the network of "associates" giving Gold Bond stamps. Homemakers earned high-ticket premiums, even mink coats. Busy at a grand opening is Curt's brother, Dean (lower photo, far left), who advanced to vice president. Curt (in circle) realized goods appealed to housewives more than cash and opened redemption centers. Gold Bond's catalog eventually carried 1,500 items.

"Sandy Saver," an impish Scottish promoter of trading stamps, was the symbol of Gold Bond Stamps at company headquarters on Hennepin Avenue in downtown Minneapolis. Carlson moved his operations to the Minneapolis suburb of Plymouth in 1962 and began to implement diversification. By this time, the nation was stamp-saturated; 19 of the top 20 supermarket grocery chains offered trading stamps.

FOSHAY
STANDARD
STANDARD
SERVICES
STANDARD
GOLD BOND STAMPS
100 FREE
DE-ICER now in RED CROWN, too!

THERE'S GOLD TO MINE
IN '49

A recent Gold Bond innovation offers trading stamps at truckstops under a program called Gold Country USA. The trading stamp concept — which has spread to Canada, Asia, and Europe — is one of the most successful and enduring promotional ideas in marketing history. Major credit goes to Curt Carlson (right) who prides himself on being a sales-man first, foremost and always. "Selling is not something you learn in school," he says. "It's a gift, like having perfect pitch or a photographic memory." He tells employees: "Nothing happens here until we sell it!"

Gold Bond Stamps spread from "mom and pop" grocery stores to other merchants. Carlson and a colleague were bolting up a Gold Bond sign at a Standard Oil station like the one (top left) on a Sunday morning in December, 1941, when word came of the Japanese attack at Pearl Harbor. World War II rationing of some groceries put Gold Bond's progress "on hold." But after the war (left), the sales force geared up for trading stamp business again with marketing mottoes flying high. Curt Carlson, who started Gold Bond at age 24, stands at far right.

Consumers could even obtain Gold Bond trading stamps for buying a used car, as illustrated by this Minnesota newspaper advertisement.

Carlson, assisted by super-salesman "Sandy Saver," breaks ground in 1961 for what would become world headquarters. Carlson bought 1,000 acres of suburban farmland west of Minneapolis where a freeway was to be built. In 1989, a new world headquarters for Carlson's private empire will rise on part of this property.

Specific and measurable goals — together with strategies for achieving them — have always been a Carlson trademark. As a young soap salesman, Curt carried a slip of paper in his wallet to remind him of his goal to earn $100 weekly plus salary. Later, personal goals became company targets for Gold Bond Stamps and diversified Carlson Companies. In 1946, key salesmen mapped out a five-year plan to expand into seven midwestern states and sell 200,000 pads of Gold Bond trading stamps, each representing $1 in profit. In 1953 Super Valu, America's largest wholesale grocery company, signed up with Curt and the big breakthrough was accomplished. Thereafter, major food chains doing business in every state gave Gold Bond stamps and the love affair between them and the American housewife blossomed.

Kenneth Carlson

Dean Carlson

Warren Carlson

Dwight Miller

Fay McCall

Dee Kemnitz

Frank Larsen

Ann Richardson

V. E. "Mac" McCoy

Joe Hunt

Orville Hammer

John Heim

Mary Golfus

Dulyn Butler

Lloyd Thompson, Jr.

H. Glendon Johnson

H. W. Greenough

Maury Gold

Chester "Chet" Krause

Warren Lorenz

Pioneer Builders
of Gold Bond

The men and women pictured on the left page were among those Carlson employees who helped to build the Gold Bond Trading Stamp Company and played key roles in the foundation of what today is Carlson Companies, Inc. Curt Carlson says in tribute: "Without people like these — of dedication and drive and stamina — a business like ours would have failed long ago. Indeed, they were pioneer builders."

Right: With his typical flair for the dramatic, Curt and his top executives in the early Sixties unfurl the pages of a Gold Bond Stamp catalog on a football field. Today, Gold Bond stamps are part of the Carlson Promotion Group. Its sister group, the Carlson Marketing Group of companies, is the largest motivational, training, marketing and incentive travel organization in the world. It all started 50 years ago on "sheer guts, $50 borrowed capital and little gummed pieces of paper" — trading stamps.

East met West in 1968 when Gold Bond Stamp Company introduced Gold Star and Gift Bond trading stamps throughout Japan in joint venture with Mitsubishi, the industrial giant. Pictured with Japanese host and hostesses, Curt Carlson is flanked left and right by Gold Bond executives Frank Larsen and Ed Brennan, both now retired.

The Japanese are avid golfers. Taking advantage of the manicured Carlson Companies' Minnesuing Acres course are T. Hirota and Peter Hamaguchi, top executives of Japanese companies affiliated with Mitsubishi and Gold Bond Japan in the Far East.

Kimono-clad hostesses prepare to welcome the board of directors of Gold Bond Japan in an alternate year when the meeting is held in Tokyo. Several Gold Bond representatives from Carlson Companies fly in from the United States. As a purchase-incentive idea, trading stamps have proved enormously popular with the Japanese consumer.

Gold Bond Japan is guided by a board of directors composed of executives from Mitsubishi, Japan's industrial giant, K. K. Hiroya, and Carlson Companies, Inc. They meet in alternate years in Japan and the United States. Here they are at Minnesuing Acres Training Facility, Carlson's business retreat in the north woods of Wisconsin. **First row (seated):** Kenneth Gudorf, vice president, finance, and chief financial officer, Carlson Companies, Inc.; Edwin C. "Skip" Gage, president and chief operating officer, Carlson Companies, Inc.; Tom Aizawa, executive vice president, Mitsubishi; H. W. Greenough, vice chairman, Carlson Marketing Group, Inc. **Second row (standing):** T. Hirota, vice president, K. K. Ryoshoku; Jim Carlson, vice president and chief financial officer, Gold Bond Japan, Ltd.; Peter Hamaguchi, president, K. K. Hiroya; Kei Nagatani, president, Gold Bond Japan, Ltd.; Mike Niida, senior assistant to managing director (Food), Mitsubishi; Tak Otake, manager, Foods, project and development department, Mitsubishi; Ray Hegre, vice president, marketing, Retail Marketing Division, Carlson Marketing Group. The partnership between Carlson and Mitsubishi is successful and expanding into other joint ventures.

Transition

The Thirties

From little acorns mighty oaks grow. The trading stamp business that Curt Carlson founded in 1938 — working first with neighborhood grocery stores like this one — formed the roots for the network of business enterprises that would blossom into Carlson Companies, Inc. Carlson celebrates 50 years of continuous growth and expansion in 1988.

J B. Say, the French economist who coined the term "entrepreneur," wrote in the year 1800: "The entrepreneur shifts economic resources out of an area of lower and into an area of higher productivity and greater yield." In the late 1950s, Curt Carlson was forced to face the truth of this wisdom.

Carlson was still succeeding with Gold Bond trading stamps but they were beginning to peak as a sales promotion tool. The handwriting was on the wall. "We could see that we couldn't continue to reach our five-year goals. Nineteen of the top 20 food market chains, and half the service stations, were giving trading stamps. So we knew we had to diversify."

C arlson chose two areas: real estate and hotels. "We already knew something about real estate because we had 330 Gold Bond Gift Centers along with nine warehouses in the U.S. and Canada." In the 1950s and 1960s, Curt Carlson bought 1000 acres of suburban farmland west of Minneapolis — the sites today of Carlson Companies' world headquarters and the future Carlson Center — and about the same time, the opportunity arose to purchase five percent of the original Radisson Hotel.

The Radisson dominated downtown Minneapolis. Owner Tom Moore had air-conditioned the hotel and added some rooms. Needing capital, he offered five percent to ten investors, including Carlson. "So we all became innkeepers. We weren't making much money but we got preferred seating in the famous Flame Room, which attracted big-name entertainers." One by one, the original investors dropped out and soon Carlson owned 50 percent and was Moore's full partner. A year later, Moore sold out to Carlson.

Hotels appealed to Carlson. The Radisson hotel was a solid piece of property with a prestigious reputation and Carlson was sure he could make it more profitable. "The best hotel gets the most business," says Carlson. "We knew we had a great name in Radisson — one we felt could be successfully expanded by building and acquiring more hotel properties. Also, when you have a number of hotels, you can become more efficient. We bought and refurbished some older hotels. However, travelers tend to patronize new properties more readily.

So now Carlson was in hotels, real estate and other incentive businesses and Gold Bond Stamp Company was no longer an appropriate name for the Carlson businesses. "We submitted the problem to some logo experts in New York," Carlson remembers. 'What would be a natural transition to another company name?' we asked. One finding was that people have confidence in a company which carries the owner's name, particularly if he is well known and respected in the community. So, in 1973, we became Carlson Companies."

In the 1970s, Carlson expanded his real estate and hotels, acquired restaurants, invested in jewelry, home building, leasing, wholesale foods, motivational systems, promotional merchandise and other businesses. Meantime, Edwin C. "Skip" Gage was quietly building up the marketing group over which he had been promoted to president. Travel, sales promotion and motivation was the new direction.

In 1983, Carlson Companies entered a new phase which Gage — now president and chief operating officer of Carlson Companies — calls "strategic focusing." Some of the companies which failed to fit the corporate matrix were sold off and the young new management team concentrated on building up company strengths. Acquisitions remained a part of corporate strategy but now were focused on related companies that would complement the businesses in which Carlson had experience and a proven track record. The search for synergistic advantage was a new element of transition.

The Eighties

Carlson Companies new World Headquarters at Carlson Center is an architecturally striking symbol of Carlson Companies today and for the 21st century. Structure is expected to open in 1989 and will anchor the total $650 million Carlson Center. Carlson Center is about a 10 minute drive from downtown Minneapolis and travers Minnetonka and Plymouth, Minnesota.

Carlson Companies is in perpetual transition and evolution. As Peter Drucker, dean of management philosophers, writes: "Entrepreneurs see change as the norm and as healthy. Usually they do not bring about the change themselves. But — and this defines the entrepreneur — the entrepreneur always *searches* for change, *responds* to it, and *exploits* it as an opportunity."

Corporate Staff

One of Carlson Companies' mottoes is "Growing and Going Globally." More than a motto, it is a reflection of the special teamwork that exists between top corporate management in Minneapolis headquarters and the diverse operating companies.

Carlson Companies is not a holding company and is not a public corporation listed on the stock exchange. Rather, it is the parent organization of a diversified family of 75 corporations, most of them operating companies in the businesses of hospitality, travel, sales promotion, motivation/marketing and real estate investments.

Corporate staff provides important logistical and management resources for the operating companies in financial management and control, data processing and information services, legal, tax, personnel, employee benefits, public relations/public affairs and administration. Corporate-level executives are intimately involved in the success of the operating companies in the field.

Curt Carlson says the "team at the top" carries a heavy load of responsibility, including the following: (1) Furnishing needed capital for improvement, growth and expansion (2) Budgetary planning and control (3) Providing legal services and (4) Setting goals and quotas with agreement and cooperation of the operating company heads.

"We believe in setting goals," says "Skip" Gage, "and establishing specific objectives to reach those goals. Agreement on goals between corporate management, operating company management and key operating unit employees is essential. These must be consistent and understood at all three levels in order to be accomplished."

Gage adds that top management must resist being "ivory tower" strategic thinkers and actively participate in the businesses. "We get out in the field to understand grassroots problems and help turn them into opportunities. It's amazing how much top management can learn from rank-and-file employees. They really know the business. But you have to take them seriously and listen."

It's a constant "balancing act," says Gage, between centralized management and decentralized control in the operating companies. "Our philosophy has been to centralize functions where there are significant advantages of specialized expertise — such as legal, tax and financial services — or in economies of scale such as in data processing and information services. Under our new configuration in businesses that have synergistic relationship, there's an almost day-to-day interchange between operating units and corporate staff."

Ann Richardson, Carlson's first administrative assistant and now vice president of administration, believes that good communication between top management and the operating companies is essential to success. "Employees must feel that they understand the company's mission, where they fit in and how they can contribute. That requires skill and sensitivity in keeping them informed and motivated. You must do this in various ways, on a regular and dependable basis, and show concern for the workers' well being."

Women at the top, left: Ann Richardson, vice president, administration and president, CSA Inc. design firm; Dee Kemnitz, vice president, employee benefits; and Doris Campbell, Carlson's executive assistant.

Legal Department — Front: Lee Bearmon, vice president, secretary and general counsel; second row: Mary Ellen O'Brien, Dick Shinofield; third row: Robert Berkwitz, Gary Widell and Gerald Hogan. Not shown: Richard Porter.

Financial Department executives (left to right): John M. Dignan, controller; John M. Diracles, Jr., treasurer; Robert Miller; Bruce M. Stevens, vice president, ISD; and Kenneth F. Gudorf, chief financial officer.

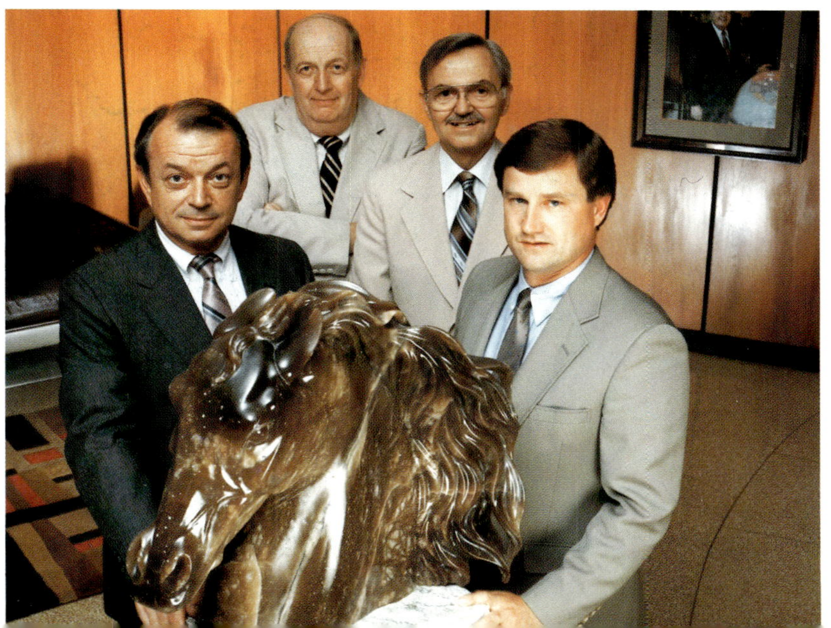

Other corporate executives (from left): Terry Butorac, Carlson Companies personnel; Thomas D. Jardine, public relations/public affairs; Kurt E. Retzler, acquisitions; and Doug Ziemer, personnel, Carlson Travel Group. All work in Minneapolis headquarters.

Hospitality

HOTEL RADISSON, MINNEAPOLIS, MINN.

Chicago heiress Edna Dickerson built this $1.5 million Radisson Hotel in 1909, naming it after the 17th-century French explorer of Minnesota, Pierre Esprit Radisson. Advertisements of the period show a room rate of $1.50; rooms with bath were $2.50. Six U.S. presidents, movie stars, and other celebrities slept here.

Carlson Companies marked a proud milestone in 1987 with the opening of the elegant flagship Radisson Plaza Hotel and Plaza VII office complex in the heart of downtown Minneapolis — a national symbol of the new generation of upscale Radisson plaza hotels being operated by the company across America. It stands on the site of the original Radisson, considered the finest hotel between Chicago and the U.S. west coast when it opened in 1909.

In 1960, Curt Carlson acquired an interest in his first hotel and entered the booming hospitality business when he and a group of Minneapolis investors purchased the original Radisson in downtown Minneapolis. Two years later, Carlson became the sole owner. This was the Minnesota entrepreneur's first step into diversification as he foresaw that the trading stamp business was faced with limited growth opportunities because of market saturation.

By the early 1970s, the Radisson flag was flying above two dozen hotels, inns and resorts. This bold strategy of diversification led Carlson Companies into the restaurant business, the management of resort properties, the travel industry, marketing and motivation, sales promotion and real estate ventures. Eventually, these diversified companies became so large they separated and regrouped into the Carlson Hospitality Group, Travel Group, Marketing Group and Sales Promotion Group.

Today, the Hospitality Group under Juergen "JB" Bartels has become a major market force in the nation's hotel, restaurant and resort industries. These operations embrace Radisson Hotel Corporation, Colony Hotels and

Imploded in 1982, the Minneapolis Radisson crumbles in dust to make way for the new Radisson Plaza Hotel and Plaza VII office complex.

Investors in the 1960 purchase of the Radisson from Tom Moore (second from right) included Curt Carlson, left; former Minnesota Governor Orville Freeman; insurance executive H.P. Skoglund; bandleader Guy Lombardo and Carl Pohlad. In 1962, Carlson assumed sole ownership of the old hotel and later financed several major renovations.

A spectacular newcomer to the Minneapolis skyline is the $108 million, 36-story Plaza VII office tower/hotel complex, completed in 1987 on the site of the original Radisson Hotel. The first 16 floors form the splendid new downtown Radisson Plaza Hotel Minneapolis and floors 18 through 36 are the office complex. Separate lobbies and elevators serve the hotel and office tower, linking up with the city's pedestrian "skyway."

Resorts, TGI Friday's restaurants and Country Hospitality, Inc. which includes Country Kitchen restaurants and Country Hospitality Inns. The Hospitality Group also includes CSA Inc., one of the nation's leading design/construction corporations specializing in the hospitality industry. Collectively, these well-managed companies have annual revenues of well over $1.8 billion in 1988.

Radisson is the fastest-growing deluxe upscale hotel chain in America but Bartels is quick to point out, "We are a collection of hotels, not just a chain. We custom design lodging properties to each individual marketplace where they are located. We are champions of service. Increasingly, we are world class." In the competitive hospitality industry, the Radisson "Yes I Can" spirit and employee motivation program is turning heads. As evidence, Radisson achieved a 5-star rating from the American Association of Travel Editors as one of America's two best hotel companies in both 1986 and 1987.

The Radisson hotels have gained respect by providing deluxe hospitality across the United States, Mexico, Europe, the Pacific region, Canada, the Middle and Far East — a hotel opened recently in Beijing, China. Expanding on the international scene, Bartels has struck agreements in the past two years with SAS International Hotels of Scandinavia; Mövenpick Hotels International, a hotel chain headquartered in Switzerland; Park Lane Hotels International, headquartered in Hong Kong and San Francisco; Banamex in Mexico and Commonwealth Hospitality in Canada.

In 1983, when "JB" Bartels joined Carlson Companies, Radisson had 25 hotels and five of these were promptly sold off. In the past four years, more than $2 billion of Radisson hotels joined the system to reach a total of 175 properties. An additional $960 million of Radisson and Colony hotels are under construction. Pursuing its strategy of aggressive growth through management contracts and by franchising, the company has the ambitious goal of 215 hotels by the end of 1988. Franchising has been a major thrust for Radisson; about 75 percent of all Radissons are franchise operations and about 25 percent are owned or operated by Carlson Companies.

Radisson's "Collection" ranges from plaza hotels to suite hotels, inns and resort properties. Another dimension of the Hospitality Group is provided by Colony Hotels and Resorts, a specialized operator of distinctive hotels, inns, resorts and condominium properties at more than 30 locations in the Hawaiian Islands and at selected travel destinations in the continental United States. Colony's Hawaiian operations include magnificent seaside resorts in paradise-like settings on Maui, Kauai, Oahu, Hawaii and Molokai. In the continental United States, Colony's operations include hotel and resort properties in a number of well-known recreational resorts and commercial centers.

TGI Friday's is one of the phenomenal success stories of the highly competitive restaurant business. Creative menus, fresh-daily foods, service with smiles and flair, distinctive decor, and a youthful ambience make the more than 150 Friday's and Dalts locations the nation's most popular dining-out and meeting places. Carlson Companies bought Friday's in 1975; since then, annual sales have increased 35 times. One key to success is young, well trained employees and managers who take pride in being on a winning team; they attract not only customers but

Radisson Mark Plaza Hotel.

The Radisson Plaza Hotel Orlando had its Florida opening in 1985. On hand were Juergen Bartels (left), president of the Carlson Hospitality Group, and John A. Norlander, president of Radisson Hotel Corporation. Radisson is the fastest-growing upscale hotel "collection" in the world and has a growth goal of 215 hotels by the end of 1988.

Carlson Hospitality executives (lower left): **Seated** *— John Norlander and Juergen Bartels.* **Second row, from left** *— William Brose, Robert Zambreno, Thomas Polski, Jack Burnett, Ken Hlavek, Robert Pearce, Harris Parmele, Blaine Wilkinson, John Olsen.* **Back row, from left** *— Keith Irlbeck, Jay Witzel, Peter Blyth, William Speidel, Scott Heintzeman, Randy Clifton, James Olson, and John Craddock. Not present in photograph are Don Clawson, Sue Gordon, Edwin (Ted) Theobald and Harriet Peterson.*

Concierge staff on the plaza floor of the new Radisson Plaza Hotel in downtown Minneapolis includes supervisor Mary Byron (seated) and (standing, from left) Teri Holte, Michelle Kaluza and Dawn Givans.

other promising personnel. TGI Friday's is the only publicly-held subsidiary of Carlson Companies, with the initial stock offering taking place in 1983. The company's stock is traded on the New York Stock Exchange. The chain is expanding rapidly and includes an exciting group of restaurants called Dalts — a modern version of the popular 1940s-style bar and grill.

Country Hospitality, Inc. is a nationwide franchised restaurant and inn chain with more than 260 locations in the U.S. and Canada. It includes Country Kitchen restaurants serving the family dining market with value-oriented, high-quality menu items, home-style cooking, and comfortable, informal surroundings. It also includes Country Hospitality Inns, a new chain offering low rates and attractive country-style lodging.

One of the first hotels built by Carlson was the Radisson Hotel South and Executive Tower in Bloomington, a Minneapolis suburb.

CSA, Inc., founded by Ann Richardson while acting as administrative assistant to Curt Carlson, has become one of the nation's foremost interior design companies. CSA frequently manages the planning and design of new and renovated hotels and restaurants for Carlson Companies. This synergistic relationship adds an important dimension of expertise and service.

"The work of CSA is highly visible to the world," says Ms. Richardson, "and our design does have real impact on the success of our hospitality entities — the hotels, the restaurants, the resorts. Tasteful, functional design enhances and advances these properties and their attractiveness and utility to the consumer. We avoid 'cookie-cutter' hotels and dining establishments; part of that achievement is architecture and part is interior design. CSA teams design to fit the region, the market and our clientele. That," reminds Ms. Richardson, "requires research, creativity, hard work and special sensitivity."

Business experts predict that the hospitality and travel industries will be America's No. 1 retail business by the 21st century. Carlson Companies is positioned and motivated to serve that market with creativity, skill and a "Yes, I Can!" spirit.

In a stroke of entertainment genius, Curt Carlson introduced the Golden Strings in the Minneapolis Radisson Hotel's Flame Room on Valentine's Day, 1963. Before the live flames were extinguished when the hotel closed in 1981, the famous ensemble — nine violinists, two pianists, one bassist led by Cliff Brunzell (center) — played over 11,000 performances for more than two million music lovers.

The lobby of the Radisson University Hotel in Minneapolis is an oasis of elegant atmosphere with "Yes I Can" service on the campus of the University of Minnesota. The Radisson "collection" of hotels excels at fitting accommodations to the environment, the community and the market.

The Radisson Mart Plaza Hotel in Miami, Florida, (right), is a relaxed place for business and leisure lodging. Of Radisson's rapid expansion in the U.S. and through overseas affiliates, J.B. Bartels, Carlson Hospitality Group president, says: "The time for Radisson is now!"

Radisson

Ann Richardson is president of CSA, Inc., a nationally respected interior design company which handles Carlson hotels, restaurants and resort properties. Seated, from left: Chuck Koosmann, Nancy Cowette, John Focht, Ginny Miller. Standing, from left: Herman Crawford, Dick Sater, Darwin Klockers and Vincent Kwok. The firm offers a full range of professional services from planning and design through selection and installation of furniture, lighting, fixtures, carpeting, decorations.

The stunning new Radisson Plaza Hotel at Austin Centre, Texas, is part of a two-tower complex of offices, condominiums and shops. The hotel has 314 rooms, numerous conference rooms and assorted ballrooms. Natural light pours through the 200-foot wall and ceiling.

Below: Juergen "JB" Bartels, president of the Carlson Hospitality Group, and John Fitts, president, Colony Hotels and Resorts.

Carlson's Colony Hotels and Resorts, manages seaside condominiums, hotels and resorts in 30 locations on five Hawaiian islands and at other travel destinations in the continental United States. Colony has years of experience in dealing with owners' associations in leisure lodging.

Radisson Hotel Lynchburg,
Lynchburg, Virginia

Radisson Plaza Hotel — At Austin Centre,
Austin, Texas

Radisson Plaza Hotel Orlando,
Orlando, Florida

Radisson Suite Hotel Downers Grove,
Downers Grove (Chicago), Illinois

Radisson Suite Hotel Tucson,
Tucson, Arizona

Radisson Plaza Hotel Minneapolis,
Minneapolis, Minnesota

Radisson Plaza Hotel at Town Center,
Southfield, Michigan

The Jekyll Island Club — A Radisson Resort,
Jekyll Island, Georgia

Radisson Park Terrace Hotel,
Washington, D.C.

Radisson Hotel — Keystone at the Crossing,
Indianapolis, Indiana

Radisson Plaza Hotel and Golf Course,
Manhattan Beach (Los Angeles), California

Union Station — A Radisson Plaza Hotel,
Nashville, Tennessee

Gem of the Pacific, Honolulu's Waikiki beach lures travelers world-wide. Carlson Companies manage resort properties on Maui, Kauai, Oahu, Molokai and Hawaii under Colony Hotels and Resorts.

In Stockholm, the Radisson-affiliated SAS Strand Hotel exudes Old World charm. Radisson is allied with SAS International

Hotels in Sweden, Norway, Denmark, Austria and Kuwait.

Acapulco's Pacific-side Radisson Paraiso Hotel, one of Mexico's finest. Carlson hotel operations also extend to Canada, Europe, the Middle East and Asia/Pacific, where tourism is expanding rapidly.

Carlson Companies has an expanding hospitality industry presence in Europe.

Left: The 493-room SAS Scandinavia Hotel in Denmark's capital city of Copenhagen, a Radisson-affiliated hotel.

Right: The dramatic Hotel Côncorde La Fayette in Paris, a tourist favorite with 1,000 rooms, is Radisson-affiliated.

Far right: The "Affiliated with Radisson" symbol is spreading around the world.

Bottom right: Park Hotel Frankfurt, a Mövenpick Hotels International facility. .It was in West Germany that Juergen Bartels, now Carlson Hospitality Group president, began his career as a 16-year-old food and beverage apprentice.

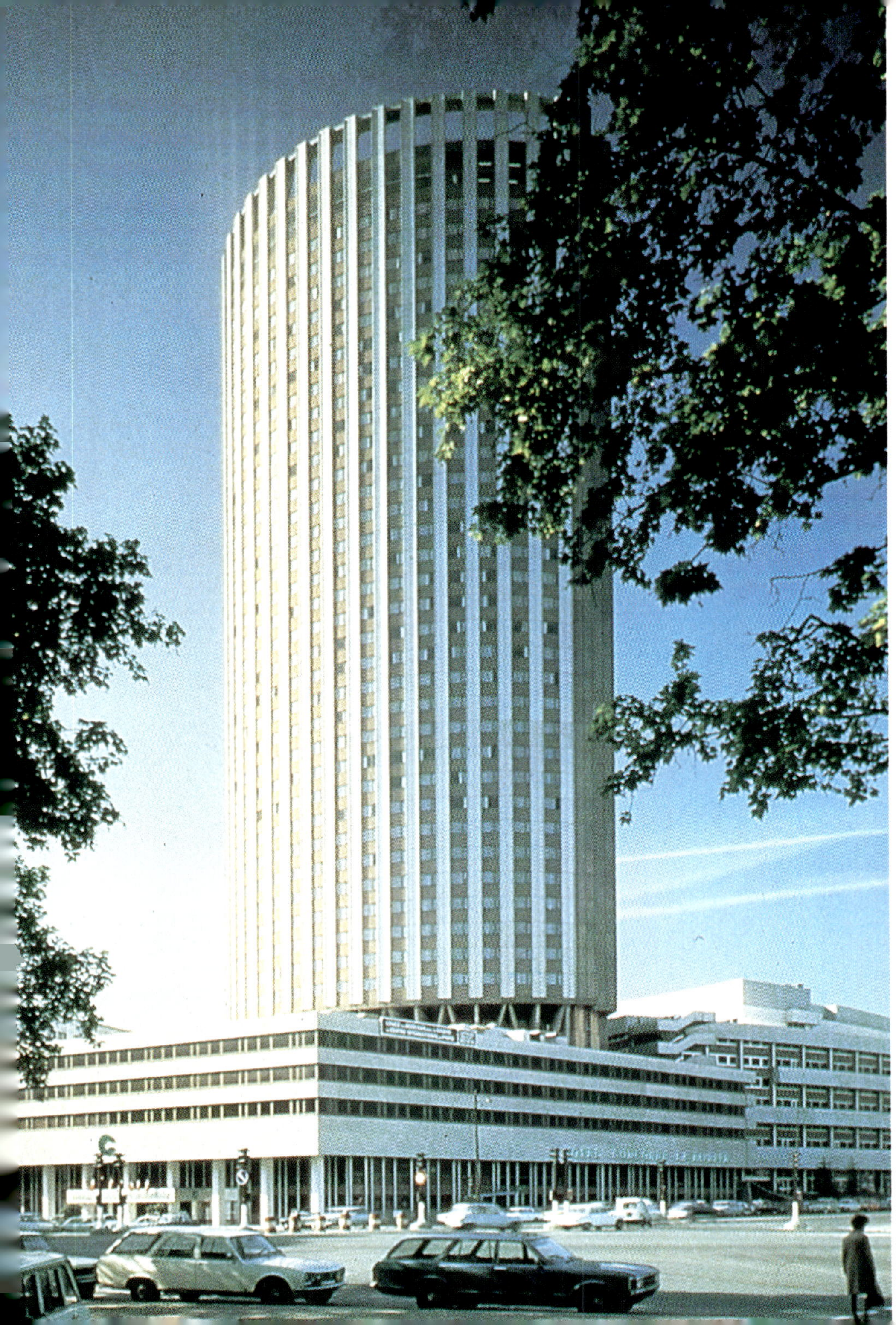

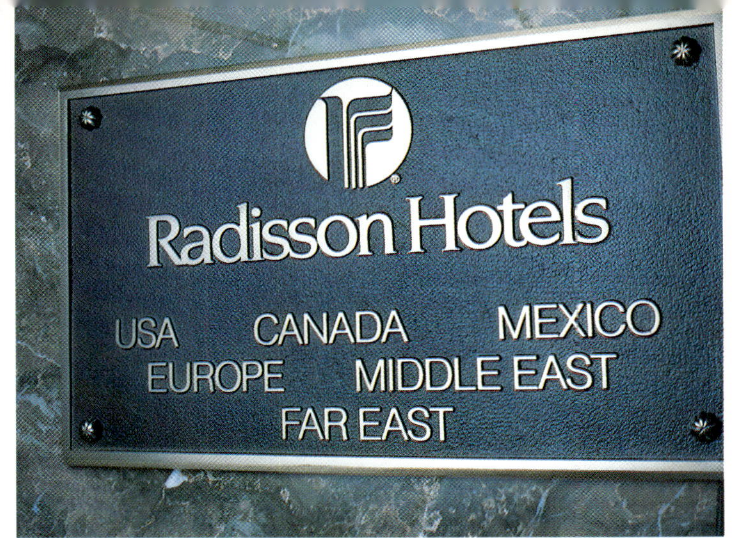

Radisson Hotels
USA CANADA MEXICO
EUROPE MIDDLE EAST
FAR EAST

Parkhotel Frankfurt
CASABLANCA BAR

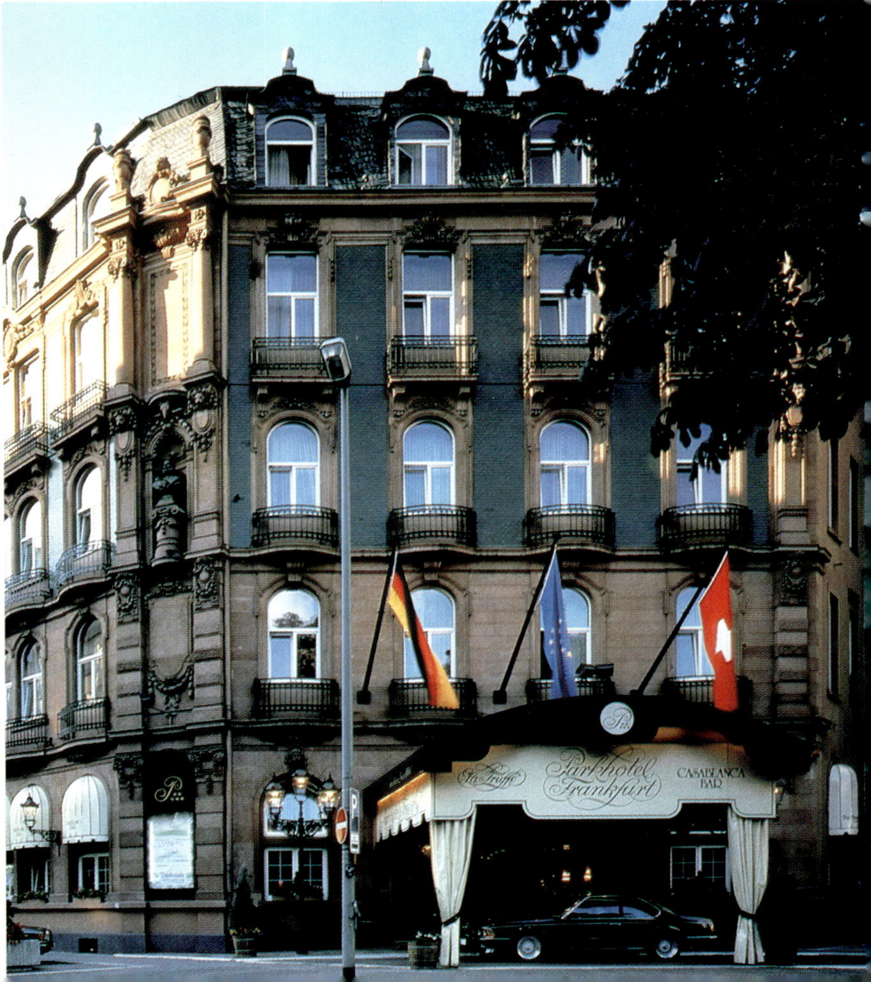

Kids get balloons as an extra attraction at TGI Friday's restaurants. Adult customers enjoy varied, creative menus, freshly prepared food and attentive service in an attractive, friendly environment. Carlson acquired TGI Friday's in 1975; in December, 1983, 4.5 million shares of the restaurant's stock (25 percent) went on the New York Stock Exchange and sold out in one day. Today, there are over 140 locations nationwide and in the United Kingdom.

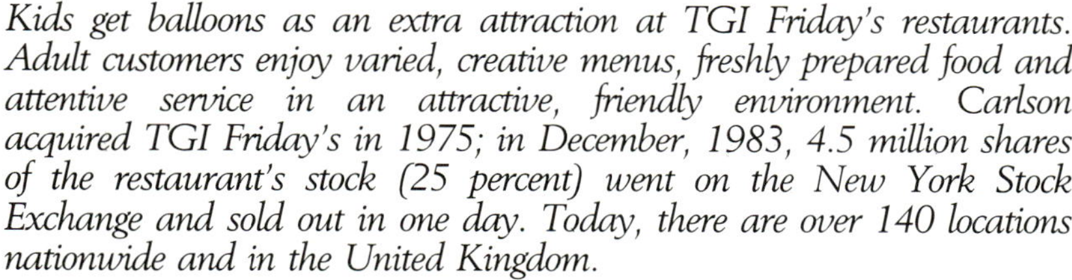

TGI Friday's executives, left to right, front row, Michael O'Donnell, Juergen Bartels, president, Hospitality Group; Left to right, second row, Nicholas S. Galanos, J. Michael Jenkins, president, TGI Friday's; and Richard Rivera. Not shown are Michael Woodhouse, David G. Short, Didier A. Peyron and Holly J. Young.

TGI Friday's success formula is a quality dining experience in clean and wholesome surroundings. Right: The two-story telephone booth is a conversation piece at most TGI Friday's locations around the country.

Dining out has mushroomed into the great American pastime for all ages, and TGI Friday's makes sure the experience is worth repeating soon. Special ambience is created with hundreds of antiques, stained glass windows, brass artifacts, live plants and an oak bar.

In addition to the turn-of-the-century atmosphere in the typical TGI Friday's, Carlson's Hospitality Group has developed other restaurant concepts. Dalts offers the consumer an inexpensive dining-out experience in a modern version of a 1940s-style bar and grill.

"Cozy and comfy" in a Country Kitchen booth, clockwise from lower left, are "JB" Bartels, Larry Danielski, John Olsen, Quint Hanson, Allan Post, Barbara Weinstein and Richard Hohman, president, Country Hospitaly, Inc.

Country Kitchen restaurants hold special appeal for the family market. Emphasis is on good food at reasonable prices and friendly "down-home" service in a setting of country-style decor and cleanliness. Acquired by Carlson in 1979, Country Kitchen is a franchised chain with more than 260 locations in the U.S. and Canada.

"Country Hospitality Inn" is a welcome sign at the end of a long day's drive. Country Hospitality Inns are being introduced to provide economy family lodging with a home atmosphere and a fireplace. Often, there's a Country Kitchen restaurant right next door. This new Country Hospitality Inn is in Burnsville, Minnesota, a Minneapolis suburb.

Ask Mr. Foster Travel was started 100 years ago in St. Augustine, Florida, by Ward Foster, whose hobby was railroad schedules and tourist information. When travel help was needed, people said "Ask Mr. Foster." Today, over 500 outlets in the U. S., Mexico bear his name.

Travel

The statistics of human travel — for business and pleasure — stretch the imagination, not to mention the social and economic implications of travel. Consider that on any one day, 15 million Americans are traveling somewhere at least 100 miles from their homes. And of this number, some 8 million Americans take a seat in a jetliner and buckle up to fly somewhere. The Wright brothers would be proud — and amazed.

For Carlson Companies, the fact that travel is projected to be one of the world's biggest industries before the century is over

Travel Group executive team includes (front row, left): John Powell, P. Lawson Travel of Canada; John Ueberroth, president, Carlson Travel Group and Travis Tanner, president, Retail Travel. Back row: Hans de Lange, Ronald Smith and Charles Benisch. Not shown: William Slattery. All four are U.S. area officers, Ask Mr. Foster Travel Service.

Carlson Companies advanced boldly into the travel business with the 1979 acquisition of Ask Mr. Foster travel agencies from the Ueberroth brothers. John, at left, became president of Carlson Travel Group and Peter, second from right beside "Skip" Gage, became 1984 U. S. Olympic organizing chairman and later, Commissioner of Baseball. The deal eventually made Carlson Travel the largest in North America.

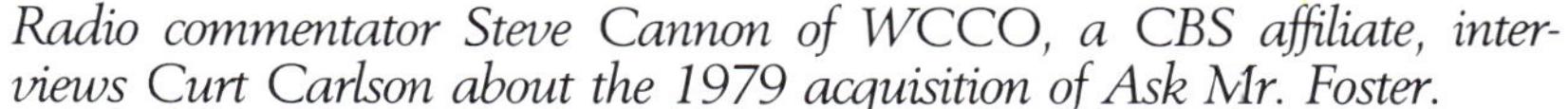

Below: In 1983, Carlson Companies acquired P. Lawson Travel Ltd., Canada's leading travel agency, with headquarters in Toronto.

Radio commentator Steve Cannon of WCCO, a CBS affiliate, interviews Curt Carlson about the 1979 acquisition of Ask Mr. Foster.

means opportunity and challenge. The Carlson Travel Group of companies, led by John Ueberroth, ranks as the largest travel organization in North America. More than 3,000 travel professionals serve consumers of leisure and business travel in retail, commercial, wholesale tours and association travel operations. "There's a will to see the world," says Ueberroth, "and I don't see it diminishing."

The deregulation of the U.S. airline industry, coupled with a surge in almost all segments of the travel business, triggered Carlson Companies' aggressive growth. Through strategic acquisitions and expansion of existing operations, the company has strengthened its position of leadership. The Carlson travel advantage is found in its dedication to consumer satisfaction, its ongoing diversification and its sheer size.

"In our Ask Mr Foster travel agencies and the other Carlson Travel Group companies," says Ueberroth, "we are growing faster and better than our competitors. Our revenues increased from less than $500 million in 1983 to over $2 billion in 1987. We're No. 1, ahead of American Express and Thomas Cook, and our size makes it possible to be more efficient. Moreover, our purchasing power translates into lower fares, better services and other extras that benefit our customers. In today's competitive market, 90 percent of air fares are discounted. Our corporate and leisure customers need all the help they can get to be sure they get the maximum discounts. As our new motto for Ask Mr Foster says, 'You can expect the world of us'."

The most visible part of Carlson Companies travel business is seen in over 600 travel agencies and outlets operating in the

Independence Day 1986 and Lady Liberty stands center stage for the world's biggest fireworks show. Curt Carlson's father and grandparents passed this way as Swedish immigrants exactly 100 years earlier, seeing the statue the year President Grover Cleveland dedicated it.

U.S., Canada and Mexico under the names Ask Mr. Foster and P. Lawson.

The U.S. companies include Ask Mr. Foster Travel Service, Ask Mr. Foster Associates, Cartan Tours and Firstours. A department store division markets upscale leisure travel in such retail stores as Neiman-Marcus. In Canada, P. Lawson Travel is the leading travel agency with more than 100 retail outlets.

Cartan Tours, Inc. is widely recognized as the leader in the wholesale travel industry with its deluxe collection of escorted tours to the world's most appealing tourist destinations. Once these were mainly Hawaii and Canada; increasingly, they are Africa and India and China. Firstours creates and markets value-priced independent vacation packages to Las Vegas, Hawaii, Mexico and other resort and world-class cities.

Commercial travel is a rapidly-growing segment of the industry. Ask Mr. Foster and P. Lawson have emerged as national leaders in the U.S. and Canada with their exclusive Business Travel Management system offering such services as guaranteed lowest airfares, 24-hour toll-free assistance hotline, consolidated billings, and management reports for budgetary control.

In 1986, each of 33 million business travelers spent $2,000 for fares, meals, hotels and car rentals. "The average corporation has a budget line item for travel and entertainment that reads at least $1 million," says Ueberroth, "and when they can save 10 percent by better control, monitoring, and leveraging their buying power, that's pure profit. The travel and hospitality world is complex — about 29,000 travel agents and 27 million hotel rooms to bargain for. We make deals. We package all this and save companies a lot of money. And because only big travel companies like ours can offer hi-tech services, smaller travel agencies are joining us as associates."

Chicago "invented" the skyscraper. Sears Tower, shown above, is the world's tallest building. Chicago has lush public parks along Lake Michigan, the world's busiest airport and is a magnet for conventions and trade shows, many of which Carlson affiliates plan and stage.

ELLIS ISLAND MEDAL OF HONOR TO CARLSON

Curt Carlson and entertainer Victor Borge were among 56 distinguished Americans honored with the Ellis Island Medal of Honor during 100th anniversary celebrations. Each winner represented one nation's immigrants.

Carlson travel consultants plan trips to Florida, Disney World, Epcot Center and other spots appealing to families, sunlovers and sportsmen.

Across friendly borders, Mexico offers tourists colorful history and culture. In season: bullfights. All year: adventure and relaxation.

Glittering Las Vegas — a neon-lit and never-sleeping desert oasis — pulsates with world-class nightlife and gambling in lavish hotels.

Inland cruises on the Mississippi and other rivers are a popular way to vacation. Mark Twain piloted paddlewheelers like this.

Incentive travel, a time-tested method of motivating employees and rewarding performance, is an important part of Carlson's travel business. Experience shows that salespeople and other employees will strive harder for an exotic vacation trip than for any other reward — including money.

E.F. MacDonald Motivation and the Carlson Travel Group — both Carlson Companies entities — are major suppliers of travel planning and operational support for some of the most sophisticated consumers of incentive and commercial travel.

Curt Carlson himself knows well the value of the travel incentive and uses it to spur excellence in his corporate leadership. In 1977, Carlson startled his top executives by promising them a trip around the world if they increased annual sales from $775 million to reach the company's first billion-dollar-year by 1981. Sparked by the global tour challenge, they reached the ambitious goal three years ahead of schedule. Using his own top travel and incentives experts, Carlson planned a trip that took his executives and their spouses on a seven-nation, ten-city dream tour in 18 days. Half of the "billion-dollar orbiters" traveled east and the other half west; they met in Tokyo for a victory celebration. Curt Carlson, flying direct from the People's Republic of China, where U.S. President Jimmy Carter sent him on a trade mission, told the happy throng of plans to operate Radisson hotels in mainland China.

Carlson is a great believer in travel, agreeing with author John Steinbeck, who wrote: "Quite apart from the fact that they leave their savings wherever they go, tourists are very valuable in the modern world. It's very difficult to hate people you know."

Travelers still leave their hearts in San Francisco, and Carlson travel consultants help them collect memories of the Golden Gate Bridge, cable cars on steep hills, seafood at Fisherman's Wharf, shopping and people-watching at the Cannery and Ghirardelli Square.

The travel delights of traditional London, the spectacular scenery and beaches at Rio de Janeiro, and the glory that was Rome — all are within reach of most tourists. Saving for these trips may be needed but memories linger on long after the last charge-card bill is paid. Carlson's Travel Group is dedicated to helping people go special places to conduct business, relax and enjoy leisure. The Group includes Cartan Tours, Inc., America's premier escorted tour company. Cartan is a leader in arranging deluxe itineraries to vacation spots in Europe, North and

South America, Asia and the Pacific. Altogether, Cartan Tours, Firstours, Ask Mr. Foster travel agencies in the U.S., and P. Lawson travel outlets across Canada do more than $2 billion in annual revenues. President Ronald Reagan said: "The tourist business is extremely important to the United States, contributing to employment, economic prosperity and international trade and understanding. Each of us benefits. It substantially enhances our personal growth, education, and appreciation of geography, history and culture."

As tourists venture out for more exotic travel destinations, eyes turn increasingly to Australia, New Zealand, South Pacific islands and the Far East. Sydney's soaring Opera House is a striking symbol of the pioneering spirit, giant land and friendly folks "down under."

Leisure Travel

The ease, speed and economy of world travel is a miracle — and a megatrend — of modern times. Travel and tourism has mushroomed into the third-largest retail business in the United States and has become a major force in the global economy. Business analysts predict it will be No. 1 before the turn of the century.

Within Carlson Companies, skilled men and women in several affiliated firms assist the business and leisure traveler in reaching and enjoying major cities and vacation destinations throughout America and around the world. The knowledge and courtesy of Carlson-affiliated travel agents and consultants pay dividends long remembered after luggage stickers are removed back home. There's a big, wide wonderful world out there and more people are exploring it.

With the opening of China, travelers are signing on for escorted tours such as those arranged by Carlson-affiliated Cartan Tours. Carlson recently opened a Radisson hotel in Beijing, the capital city, which is crawling with commerce, industry and tourism.

Below: Cruise vacations arranged by Carlson-affiliated travel companies traverse the seven seas. Especially popular with the leisure market are carefree voyages to the sun-splashed Mexican Riviera, Caribbean, Panama Canal, South Pacific, Asia and Scandinavia.

Incentive Travel

Travel — not cash bonuses — is the most popular and effective incentive used to motivate superior performance of salespeople, dealer organizations and employees generally. As one writer put it: "Nothing increases productivity like a good whiff of jet fuel."

A billion-dollar-plus industry, incentive travel is one of the fastest-growing segments of both the incentive and travel businesses. The insurance industry is a top user and so are the industries of parts, tires and accessories, cars and trucks, office equipment and cosmetics. And while more sales volume is a major objective, incentive travel is also used to encourage employees to increase manufacturing productivity, suggest cost savings ideas, stop waste, improve safety records and even build better attendance and punctuality.

Incentive travel represents a special form of recognition for superior performance. One reason it works so well is that spouses have a stake in the results. One salesperson asked his company to stop sending "report cards" home. All the spouse wanted to talk about over ham and eggs in the morning was, "How are we doing on winning that trip to Hawaii?"

On land and sea, plaid-jacketed trip directors of E. F. MacDonald's incentive travel make touring easy with exacting attention to detail.

In 1979, Curt Carlson rewarded his top executives and their spouses with a whirlwind around-the-world tour for achieving their first $1 billion year in revenues. A favorite tour guide was Ajchara Vithyanond, (left), who shepherded the group around Bangkok, Thailand, and its rich treasures of temples, gardens and canals. Right: In 1983, Carlson executives visit Egypt and the Ramses II statues at Abu Simbel, moved from Nubian temples where the Aswan dam now forms a lake on the lower Nile. Carlson took his executives to Australia in 1988.

America's leading corporations rely on Ask Mr. Foster to guide their employees through a maze of airports, hotels and car rental systems. Ask Mr. Foster and P. Lawson in Canada have emerged as national leaders in this field with their exclusive Business Travel Management system, offering such special services as guaranteed lowest airfares, a 24-hour tollfree assistance hotline, consolidated billings and detailed reports for commercial travel and entertainment budget controls.

Commercial Travel

Time was when the traveling business executive phoned the airlines for tickets, the hotel chain for reservations, and the car rental agency for wheels. The upper level executive had his secretary or personal travel agent do the job.

Much has changed with the increase in the volume and complexity of today's commercial travel; for example, about 90 percent of airfares are discounted. The effective executive needs fast and foolproof travel arrangements matched up with maximum savings.

Ask Mr. Foster offers comprehensive business travel management through a network of more than 500 offices in the United States and the financial capitals of Europe and the Far East. In Canada, P. Lawson offers similar services through 100 outlets.

Carlson's 3,500 travel experts utilize state-of-the-art telecommunications and reservation systems to answer incoming calls — many of them on 24-hour toll-free lines — quickly and efficiently. Ask Mr. Foster can secure seats on flights when other agencies show "sold out." An exclusive "AccuFare Plus" system, displaying domestic and international fares on computer screens, works so well that Ask Mr. Foster guarantees the lowest airfare available at the time of ticketing...or pays the difference.

At the same time, Ask Mr. Foster's Key Rate corporate hotel program has emerged as the finest in the industry — with more hotels, more cities and more "lower-than-commercial" rates than competitors. Car rentals at lowest prevailing rates are another promise to the commercial traveler.

Shell
TRAVEL
RESERVATIONS
PEARSON TRAVEL

Motivation

The history of Carlson Companies is rooted in marketing, sales promotion and motivation. With a single idea — Gold Bond trading stamps — founder Curt Carlson planted a seed that would grow and blossom into a diverse marketing empire. His original company, born of his love for selling goods and persuading people, provided the launching pad for diversification into related marketing, motivational and promotional enterprises.

The driving force was Carlson's own inner motivation — to succeed, to achieve goals, to accumulate capital for expansion and for other entrepreneurial ventures. With his raw energy and charismatic style, Curt motivated his salesmen, his managers and his small office staff. Even more important, he motivated his customers and clients to share in his success story. As he acquired new businesses, it was natural that the Minnesota-based entrepreneur would seek opportunities in the fields he knew best — marketing, motivation and communications.

Today, the Carlson Marketing Group has become the cornerstone of Carlson Companies, Inc., and the world's largest incentive, marketing, training, communications and corporate meetings organization. Under the leadership of Group President James K. Pfleider, its mission is to assist business and industry in achieving corporate objectives. Carlson Marketing Group professionals work as consultants and partners to improve business performance by motivating managers, sales personnel, employees and customers to achieve established goals in a wide range of competitive business environments.

Much of the original credit for developing the Carlson Marketing Group goes to Edwin C. "Skip" Gage. In 1968, Curt Carlson persuaded his son-in-law to join the company to build and take advantage of what both men saw as a major marketing and promotion opportunity. It was at Northwestern University that Gage met and married Barbara Carlson, Curt's younger daughter. But Gage had no interest in joining a one-dimensional family business. He and his super-salesman father-in-law were poles apart in temperament and management style. Instead, to pursue his interest in promotion and marketing, Gage decided to work for three years as an advertising executive in the Chicago office of Foote, Cone and Belding Agency. Meanwhile, Curt Carlson was patient.

Over time, and after long talks about the future direction of the company, Carlson convinced Gage to come on board as the director of market research and development. Both men felt that Gage's background in advertising and promotion might contribute to the company's momentum. At this point, Curt had branched out into hotels and was entering a period of aggressive diversification. By Carlson's own admission, he liked the "action" of acquisitions and he ventured forth like a Viking.

"Gage's presence and contributions were not clearly visible during his first decade with Carlson Companies," writes one business editor, "mostly because the organization's prodigious growth happened in an eclectic, unfocused sort of way." Gage served as a catalyst to create sharp focus.

Carlson Marketing Group includes executives of E. F. MacDonald Motivation and related companies. Front center: James K. Pfleider, group president. Second row, from left: Richard Fordyce and Peter Kenyon. Back grouping: Ken Swanton, Phil Ousley, Roy Lagenaur, Walt Erickson, Gentry Thatcher, Sr., Mike DeCamp, John Kalenberg.

Carlson Companies, Inc.
WORLD HEADQUARTERS

In the 1970s, Carlson moved into travel, restaurants, real estate, jewelry, home building, leasing, wholesale foods, employee motivational systems, promotional merchandise and other businesses. In the midst of what seemed frenetic acquisition, Skip Gage was strategically building up the marketing group over which he had been appointed president. Marketing services, motivation, training, incentive travel, merchandise and promotion were the foundation of Carlson Marketing Group.

This strategic focus became evident in 1976. At the time, Skip Gage was running the Carlson Marketing and Promotion Group. Carlson's total sales promotion and performance incentives/motivation business placed them as Number 4 in the market. Under Gage's leadership, a major decision and commitment was made to reorganize, expand, re-define the entire promotion and incentives business and leap past the competition.

Says Gage: "We knew we had to do some things differently — and much better — to move up to Number 1. So we decided to build an integrated sales promotion and motivation company which would service both the consumer promotion side and internal employee incentive side of the marketing equation. There was no real competition in this arena of full service."

Part of the strategy, starting in 1979, was to acquire and build up a retail travel operation to generate additional revenues and give Carlson a more competitive position in the incentives/travel business. This was accomplished with the acquisition of First Travel Corporation, including Firstours and the Ask Mr. Foster travel agencies.

Gage's vision of Carlson Companies as the premier full-service marketing and travel operation crystalized by 1980. Then came the 1981 acquisition of E. F. MacDonald Motivation Company — "the frosting on the cake," as Gage puts it. He personally put

Quality Service Management is a process that uses the proven principles of motivation to turn corporate cultures into customer-driven and service-oriented environments. Creating a workable plan of action requires the ongoing involvement of all levels of an organization.

in six solid months to nail down the acquisition. "The opportunity to acquire E. F. MacDonald was the perfect strategic fit for us," says Gage. "Our strategy was already in place with the concept of full service for corporations needing assistance in sales promotion, marketing and motivation. We had already become the leader in this 'quiet giant' of a business. With the acquisition of E. F. MacDonald Motivation, we seized the opportunity to become the dominant force in the industry." In 1984, Gage named James K. Pfleider president of the Carlson Marketing Group.

Pfleider has both the dynamism and the physique of a highly competitive athlete who enjoys being a winning coach. He talks about his job in tones of intensity and enthusiasm that suggest a college pep rally. He demands much of his team, they perform, and he is proud of their record. His client list reads like a "Who's Who in Business and Industry" and he believes strongly that Carlson Marketing Group must continue to rise above the standards and image normally associated with a traditional old-line "incentive house."

"We have grown and matured into a highly professional, full-service marketing agency," says Pfleider. "Carlson Marketing Group brings to the client's table a full menu of business solutions — one of the major ones being motivation. To paraphrase our mission statement, we help clients achieve their sales, marketing and communications objectives. We do this through professional consultation to arrive at the most creative plan to serve each client. And our fulfillment services are widely regarded as the best in the industry."

Using the expertise of their broad incentive, training and communications systems, Carlson Marketing Group professionals assist clients in motivating employees, customers and others throughout their marketing network to attain specific goals. "Since your success is directly related to our clients' success," Pfleider said, "we are totally customer-driven."

The flagship of Carlson Marketing Group, acquired in 1981, is E.F. MacDonald Motivation, founded in 1922 and a pioneer in the field. It grew from a luggage company in Dayton, Ohio, whose owner, Elton F. MacDonald, noticed that companies sometimes bought large quantities of suitcases and briefcases for prize-winning salesmen. Seeing an opportunity, he decided to concentrate on selling other merchandise that would be useful in increasing performance. Later, the enterprise expanded into incentive travel, training, meetings planning, commu-

Meeting planning, exhibits and trade fairs are among the diverse services which Carlson Marketing Group provides for client corporations like Shell Oil, General Motors, Navistar and AT&T. Services range from air and ground transportation to staging and entertainment.

nication products (including state-of-the-art audiovisuals), and tracking and reporting systems.

Marketing and motivation is a multi-billion dollar business, but one which is not widely recognized perhaps because it's not well understood. Part of the reason is that the emblem of E.F. MacDonald Motivation, Carlson's major division for marketing and motivation, never appears on the materials of communications used by clients. Results are seldom credited to the motivation company except by top management. The client is the focus. He arranges for the service and reaps the results.

To install an effective motivation program calls for a substantial commitment on the part of a client corporation, but it's one that more than pays the company back. The Carlson Marketing Group sales representative goes to the largest companies and says with confidence, "We can help you achieve your corporate goals — all the way from handling a sales meeting to setting up an incentive program that, when successful, will send your top performers on an exotic trip to the Orient." The job is very sophisticated and complex —— for example, serving as a full-service marketing agency for a client, with a dedicated and skilled staff handling virtually all aspects of that client's sales, marketing or communication strategy.

But an investment in motivation and marketing programs pays rather than costs, according to Pfleider. "We promise our clients and prospects that the cost of our services will be covered by incremental sales or other results of increased performance. We don't really get paid unless the program is a success. We are partners with our clients."

How does motivation work? Take an example of a bank; Carlson Marketing Group specialists have worked with many across the country. The bank's employee organization is divided into teams, each with a captain. A team might include a teller, a personal banker, a bank officer, a computer programmer and even a janitor. After the team captain is trained, the teams are taught more about the bank's objectives and long-range plans, how they can be better ambassadors for the bank and how to sell the bank's services.

The teller tells her friends and neighbors about the bank's services and the great place she works. She talks it up with her contacts in church, the PTA and with her bridge club. As a result, the bank obtains new customers — perhaps to set up a checking or savings account, apply for a loan or open a security box. The employee gets credit when she helps the bank grow and she is rewarded — with merchandise from a gift catalog or, for superior performance, perhaps with a travel award such as a Caribbean cruise.

"Such a motivation program produces measurable results," says Pfleider. "It can bring millions of dollars into a banking institution. Moreover, it builds employee morale. The bank is telling the employee: 'We want your help in selling the bank's services. We think you are very important. We want to teach you more about this bank. We want to help you be a better employee, increase your skills, and then we are going to reward you and recognize you.' *Motivation works!*"

Few major corporations try to provide in-house motivation services. It takes years of experience. For most companies it would not be cost-efficient to maintain the staff of specialists and set up the necessary training systems, communication tools, reward vehicles and performance tracking mechanisms. Carlson Marketing offers expertise that saves their clients time and money and assures the success of their programs.

Meetings are important as motivation, communication and training events, and Carlson Marketing Group's Meetings Division is expert at providing full-service resources to stage all aspects of them. Available to clients are meeting planners, multi-media audiovisual experts, set designers, scriptwriters, producers, business theater professionals, and travel and hospitality staff.

For example, Carlson Marketing Group staged a gigantic informational and inspirational meeting in Las Vegas for a group of about 6,000 dealers. Carlson Marketing Group handled all the promotional communication for the meetings, air and ground transportation, hotel arrangements, food and beverage, entertainment and the associated trade fairs with some 75 exhibits. For the huge general sessions, they handled the decoration, staging (including sound, lighting and AV support) and drafting of about 25 speeches for company executives. They created seven sets to stage various parts of the meetings. A series of these major events have been implemented by Carlson Marketing Group for this particular client. Carlson Marketing Group staff thus becomes a critical part of the client's marketing team and, in order to do a good job, the Carlson Marketing Group account executive and support team must learn as much as the top management about the objectives and plans of the corporation.

This level of service is not limited to the United States. Carlson Marketing Group International is making the global marketing of motivational methods a reality by operating in 23 countries. With local representation, the legal, currency, linguistic and cultural complexities in each country can be integrated in multinational programs. In Canada, Carlson Marketing Group, Ltd., is recognized as the foremost motivation marketing organization.

Carlson Marketing Group and Carlson Promotion Group do similar and related work but with different client groups. In Carlson Marketing Group, the goal is to motivate sales personnel, manufacturing and other employees, and dealer organizations to change and improve their performance and productivity. In Carlson Promotion Group, the target is to motivate the consumers to make purchasing decisions and to build buyer loyalty and continuity.

Skip Gage explains the relationship between marketing/motivation and sales promotion in this way: "Think of a pipeline to the consumer. In marketing, the manufacturer-dealer organization is *pushing* the product or service through the pipeline. This is done by motivating sales people by various methods — sales meetings, learning seminars, communications, recognition, merchandise and travel incentive programs. At the other end of the pipeline, sales promotion is trying to influence the consumer, *pulling* the product or service through. This is done with coupons, sweepstakes, rebate and refund programs and frequent-user incentives. Marketing, motivation and promotion are all close partners."

Learning is another important element of the motivation spectrum, and Carlson Marketing Group serves this market with Carlson Learning Company, including Performax Systems International. Utilizing advanced learning techniques, the educational specialists of the Carlson Learning Company effectively translate knowledge into improved employee productivity and better work habits and attitudes. These methods are implemented within Carlson Companies, Inc., as well as for an impressive list of Fortune 500 clients.

Pfleider tells the story of one client introducing an expensive new hi-tech truck to the market. This company needed a training and incentive program to motivate dealers to buy the trucks and sell them to their customers. "Our training people didn't know anything about trucks," says Pfleider, "but they did in-

depth interviews with company management and engineers. They wrote a complete manual on the truck, how it works, and the advantages for the user. They then conducted seminars to teach the dealers the truck's features and benefits and how to sell the truck. And all this was overlaid with an incentive program that rewarded the dealers in tangible terms for truck sales. It all comes down to an equation we believe works: Motivation times knowledge equals performance.''

Carlson Learning Company has pioneered much of the work in the training-plus-incentives area. One of the basic ways to improve productivity of any business enterprise is to increase the skill, knowledge and motivation of employees. Motivation experts are still learning how truly effective the combination of good training and well conceived motivation programs can be. The whole area of adding motivation to quality service efforts and other team-building and problem-solving efforts expands the horizons of productivity potential.

Performax, a publisher of learning instruments, produces manuals and tests to measure personality and career aptitude — how the employee is likely to fit the corporation and be able to perform his or her job. Performax materials and services are provided through a network of about 10,000 professional training consultants in cities around the world. "Our international division is now working in Canada and Europe," says Pfleider, "where there's tremendous potential. The field is especially fertile in the Far East, where training is a much bigger part of the employee productivity mix than incentives. We already do business with major multinational clients

From conception to reality, professional meeting planners of Carlson Marketing Group help some of the world's largest corporations stage meetings to motivate their dealers, salesmen and other employees. Carlson Marketing Group arranges large-scale meetings as well as seminars and skill-building training sessions for smaller groups.

who often require a single marketing and motivation program, custom-developed and implemented worldwide. We are one of the few companies that can customize a marketing plan culturally, linguistically, monetarily and legally to fit the mores and mentality of the world's vastly diverse environments.''

Carlson Marketing Group offers a full array of products and services used singly or in tandem to assist businesses and clients. Says Curt Carlson, who has often been called Mr. Motivation: "If the employee doesn't know how to do something, that's a lack of a skill. If he doesn't know what he's supposed to do, that's a lack of knowledge. If he doesn't care about what he's doing, that's a lack of motivation. In our motivation and marketing companies, we can counter all three of these problems with our programs.'' In summary, the programs include:

• *Award Systems* — motivation with a focus on carefully selected collections of fine merchandise.

• *Incentive Travel* — innovative planning and flawless fulfillment from experts with the buying power of North America's largest travel-arrangements organization.

• *Performance Tracking* — measurement systems that monitor the productivity of participants in achieving specific client objectives.

• *Corporate Meetings, Conventions, Trade Shows* — multimedia shows, travel planning and execution, learning systems and supporting materials, all skillfully managed by professional meeting planners.

• *Learning Systems* — customized training programs, seminars and instrumented learning approaches using a network of certified consultants in nearly every major city in the world.

Carlson Learning Company (Performax Systems International) is a global network of training professionals who serve the needs of business and industry. Their challenge: helping management and employees keep abreast of today's fast-track age of technology.

Recognition of excellence in performance can take the form of tangible awards. The "psychic income" awarded to high achievers is part of the motivation package that assures the continuation of superior performance.

Successful organizations communicate... with customers, with employees and within the markets they serve. Carlson Marketing Group professionals create messages that motivate increased productivity.

- *Recognition* — programs and products to give meaningful recognition to top performers in sales, safety, merit and length of service.
- *Communications* — customized programs designed to reach and influence people at all levels of business.

Working independently or in unison to meet client objectives, the companies of Carlson Marketing Group offer leading-edge resources for comprehensive marketing and effective motivation in today's ever-changing, ultra-competitive business and industrial universe.

The vast majority of Carlson Marketing Group's motivation work is sales-related but the biggest growth potential in the industry, predicts Skip Gage, will come in moving the methodology into the workplace of service industries and inside the office. "We have a new program called 'Teamworks,' which is an employee suggestion system built around the quality circles concept with an integrated reward system. Suggestion systems are not new, but this represents new and more effective packaging. A company might be divided into ten teams, each with a captain, and their objective is to come up with documentable, implementable ways to save money, cut waste and increase revenues. It's amazing how much your employees know about running your business — what you're doing wrong and what you could be doing better. Things that management should have known about and acted on years before."

"But," observes Gage, "it's not necessarily in the employees' self interest to tell you these things. So... you make it worth their while by making them feel important and by rewarding their superior performance and their teamwork. The carrot at the end of your employee suggestion system stick is an incentive program that rewards them with merchandise or perhaps

A Carlson strategy: Synergistic acquisition

A landmark event in the strategic growth of Carlson Companies came in 1981 with the acquisition of E. F. MacDonald Motivation Company, the nation's largest and most experienced marketing, motivation and incentive organization. The joining of Carlson and MacDonald is a classic example of synergistic acquisition.

With offices in more than 40 major U.S. markets, the motivation affiliate positions Carlson to contribute significantly to the productivity of almost any business, industry or association. It increases performance levels among employees, managers, dealers and sales representatives. Awards and recognition — key elements in human motivation — are packaged by professionals at E.F. MacDonald into customized performance programs.

"Skip" Gage, president and chief operating officer of Carlson Companies, explains that management embarked on a strategic acquisition plan in the 1980s with these guiding principles:

"One: We will look at markets and businesses we know something about. We had been in the marketing and sales promotion business since the early days of Gold Bond trading stamps so E.F. MacDonald fit. We'd been in travel so we acquired Ask Mr. Foster. We had experience in hotels and restaurants; hence Radisson, Colony Resorts, TGI Friday's and Country Hospitality became a part of our company.

"Two: We consider businesses where we can be a major factor in the marketplace; we won't run back in the pack behind the leaders.

"Three: We search out businesses with opportunity for growth either because the entire market is growing or because we see a chance to build our market share within the business.

It is generally accepted that the incentive business began in this Dayton, Ohio, building in 1922. Elton F. MacDonald went to work for A. C. Cappel, took over his umbrella and luggage business after Cappel's death, and built it as a top incentive company. In the '50s and '60s, MacDonald and Curt Carlson became known as the "Fathers of the Incentive Business." Carlson, who built his incentives reputation with Gold Bond trading stamps, acquired E. F. MacDonald Motivation in 1981; it is now part of the Carlson Marketing Group.

"Four: We look for businesses that historically provide the level of return on investment we require.

"And five, a key point: We look for businesses with potential for synergistic advantage — to blend with and support businesses we are already in."

"There's obvious synergy," says Gage, "between the hospitality business and both commercial and leisure travel. You fly on an airline, you stay in a hotel and you eat out. There's also synergistic effect between travel and the motivation business because free trips are the largest single reward in motivating dealers, sales people, managers and rank-and-file employees."

In 1985, *Venture* magazine ranked Carlson Companies as the 11th largest entrepreneurial company still run by its founder. Carlson's 1987 revenues of $4 billion would rank it even higher today except the list is restricted to publicly-owned companies younger than ten years. One big reason for this growth: synergistic acquisition.

an exotic vacation trip. We learned long ago that the 'jelly-bean' method of rewarding superior performance doesn't work long. People need more than a pat on the back.

"We use the 'Teamworks' approach," Gage continues, "within various entities of Carlson Companies — including our own corporate staff — and it's incredible what people will do for you if they simply know what you want and if you trust them to help you achieve it. Our selection process focuses on managers and other leaders who are achievers. Achievers care. They care about results, and not to the detriment of the people who work for them. The best managers I know create a win/win situation between the corporation and the employee. We try to select people who are goal and achievement oriented to spearhead these motivation programs. This involves a kind of entrepreneurial spirit that is truly *intra*preneurial."

Edward B. Flanagan, former president of the Sales Executives Club of New York, has written what seems to be an apt description of a Carlson Companies' marketing and motivational professional: "Nobody wants bean counters now. Corporations want marketers who know about product life cycles and how to develop product strategies. They want executives who understand that basic marketing means moving goods and services from the producer to the consumer. Ones who know which industries are growing and which are failing. How consumer lifestyles and work habits affect product choices. Executives who are wise enough to understand these changes and see new opportunities for their companies. And know how to get the job done!"

Tracking performance requires the sophistication of modern technology and the personal expertise of skilled and knowledgeable professionals.

Getting the job done is the watchword of Carlson Marketing Group. Furthermore, this family of service companies is one of huge and continuing promise in the years ahead. For Carlson Companies and for clients.

Providing focus and full-service meetings support is a Carlson Marketing Group strength. Multimedia presentations can add impact and the audiovisual department gives careful attention to detail. State-of-the-art technology and creativity maximize the client's message.

Above: Something for everyone is the delivered promise of Carlson Marketing Group travel consultants. From the bustle of Broadway to the glitter of Las Vegas, deluxe trips create memories for award winners.

Top left: London. Global marketing for multinational corporations is a complex undertaking that requires adaptation for legal, currency, lingual and cultural differences. Carlson Marketing Group, International operates in 23 countries, offering clients a full range of incentive, communications, training and consulting services.

The training of employees and others involved in marketing requires ongoing effort. The behavioral psychologists of Carlson Learning Company target a variety of objectives: product knowledge, teambuilding, productivity, sales training and customer service skills.

The importance of recognition and appreciation for performance excellence cannot be overrated — whether it's an awards banquet in a London hotel, merchandise from a gift catalog or a free vacation trip.

Motivating employees — and using top executives to recognize and reward them — is a Carlson trademark. At right, "chef" Skip Gage serves food to participants in a "Teamworks" program inaugurated to encourage employees to make suggestions to save the company time and money and to improve productivity and operational efficiency. The same "Teamworks" approach can be effectively used by other companies and is avilable through Carlson Marketing Group.

PEPSI

Beatrice

B

Holiday Inn
Priority Club

THE PROCTER & GAMBLE COMPANY
EXCELLENCE THROUGH COMMITMENT & INNOVATION
1837-1987

CITICORP ◆ DINERS CLUB

BUICK

LOWE'S

Rockwell
International

WARNER
LAMBERT

AT&T

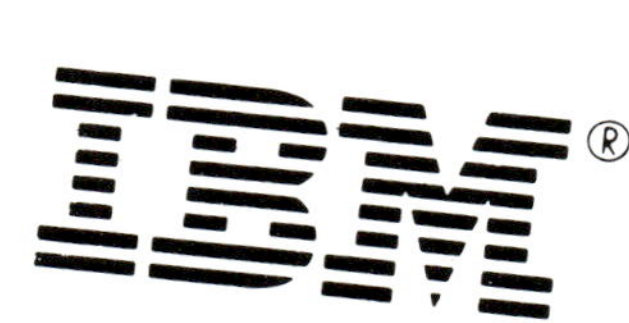
JOHN DEERE

NASH FINCH COMPANY

MOTOROLA INC.

NISSAN

Tonka

Lever

VW

IBM

OSHMAN'S

Montgomery Ward

CONOCO

VALVOLINE

The Prudential

Kimberly-Clark

TARGET

Coors

CHRYSLER
MOTORS
SERVICE & PARTS
OPERATIONS

Commonwealth
HOSPITALITY

THE ROYAL BANK
OF CANADA

Hoteles Paraíso

ARTHUR
ANDERSEN
& CO.

SAS
INTERNATIONAL
HOTELS

SAFEWAY

SUPER VALU

MAZDA

AA
American Airlines

PONTIAC
GM

Mitsubishi Corporation

MÖVENPICK
HOTELS
INTERNATIONAL

Oldsmobile

NAVISTAR

GENERAL ELECTRIC

Campbell Soup Company

CONTROL DATA

TOYOTA

Cadillac

UNITED
TECHNOLOGIES

Coca-Cola
Trade-mark ®

Delta Air Lines

BFGoodrich

General Mills, Inc.

HE DIAL CORPORATION

Sales Promotion

I f you have ever entered a promotional sweepstakes, mailed in a rebate coupon after buying a small appliance, or carried a key chain bearing a corporate logo-trademark, you have come in contact with Carlson Companies Promotion Group without knowing it.

Sales promotion efforts of these companies daily influence countless millions of consumer decisions in the American marketplace — and overseas, too. The very foundation of Carlson Companies — Gold Bond trading stamps — was a promotion and marketing idea. Curt Carlson's instinctive skill and genius in promoting continuity of purchase is reflected today in the company's leadership in the field of marketing full-service programs that stimulate sales, increase profits, and capture and keep consumer loyalty.

"The client services of Carlson Promotion Group," says Edwin C. "Skip" Gage, president and chief operating officer of Carlson Companies, Inc., "are particularly important in today's uncertain economic climate as businesses strive for identity and positioning in an increasingly competitive and deregulated economy."

"Sales promotion has gained a great deal of respectability in recent years," says Joel E. Burke, group president, "and in 1986 surpassed advertising in total revenues. It's a mega-billion-dollar business built on ideas. Sales promotion is in tune with both

Jason/Empire, Inc., is a leading importer-manufacturer of quality sporting optics, including binoculars, telescopes and rifle scopes.

Promotion Group executives include (from left): Allan Winneker of K-Promotions; Donald E. Addy, Jason/Empire, Inc.; Joel Burke, president of the Carlson Promotion Group; Thomas V. Belle of Retail Marketing and Randall Antik in Promotional Marketing.

How would you like a Doritos-brand tele-phone inside a plastic football? Fulfillment of promotional premiums, couponing, rebates and sweepstakes are big business. Carlson warehouses are loaded with watches, dolls, collectibles, cake pans and other items await-ing redemption.

Carlson is the "official licensed premium merchandise supplier" to the 1988 U.S. Olympics Committee. Logo-identified merchandise is a major sales promotion tool and comes in an almost endless profusion from key chains to coffee mugs. Carlson's K-Promotions is a nationally recog-nized leader in dealer and trade program merchandise catalogs and seat-pocket gift catalogs on airlines.

Point-of-purchase rebate coupons, sweepstakes and premium fulfillment are an almost invisible part of Carlson Companies activity since this service is for other big companies. Ideas are critical in creating product awareness. A major new trend is harnessing sales promotion for frequent-flyer, frequent-renter and frequent-sleeper programs. The Promotion Group also handles major recall campaigns such as for Tylenol.

manufacturers' short-term and long-term marketing needs. Its impact is felt quickly; sales promotion offers pinpoint target-marketing, and it is measurable. Interestingly, the Carlson trademark goes unseen, for this is a service business for major manufacturers and merchandisers.

K-Promotions, Inc., is the nation's leading supplier of logo-identified merchandise such as imprinted desk accessories, tee shirts, caps, jackets, mugs, calendars, key chains and a host of other items used to aid in marketing a brand or logo. Research proves that the positive impact of specialty promotions is powerful and enduring. K-Promotions influences airline travelers with the seat-pocket in-flight gift catalogs it produces for virtually every major U.S. carrier.

Other Carlson-affiliated companies serve consumer product firms nationwide by planning, creating and handling millions of consumer redemptions — including refunds, rebates, premiums, sweepstakes and product sampling like that little plastic container of new shampoo in yesterday's mail. "Major companies make all these promises to consumers and hire people like us to keep them,'' says Burke.

Such giant corporations as Procter & Gamble, Eastman Kodak, General Mills, and Pepsi Cola are among the many firms that initiate — and benefit from — promotions launched by the Carlson Promotion Group each year. A large staff of skilled marketing and sales promotion professionals process and track more than 100 million consumer transactions yearly.

Carlson's Promotion Group also embraces Jason/ Empire, Inc., a leading importer and marketer of sporting optics and leisure goods. The product line includes binoculars, telescopes, microscopes, magnifiers, racquetball racquets and quality sports bags. These are sold through sporting goods outlets, department stores and other mass merchandisers in the United States and Canada.

In the Carlson Promotion Group, Gold Bond's legacy lives on in trading stamps for food and drugstores and even in truckstops across America under the name of ''Gold Country, U.S.A.'' The trading stamp concept has been further refined with a promotion called ''controlled markdown'' programs which allows retailers to offer dramatic discounts on merchandise they sell.

Another new development, ''Frequent Shopper Program,'' electronically monitors consumer buying habits and enables promotion-alert retailers to reward shopper loyalty. ''With Gold Bond stamps, it was lick 'em and stick 'em,'' says Burke. ''But more and more the computer will keep score.''

Youngsters still clip coupons and send for toys. Sales promotion can make or break a new product; lack of it can cause sales of an old product to dwindle. Skilled and creative professionals in Carlson Promotion Group create, execute and measure the promotional impact of merchandising ideas. Their ''laboratory'': the competitive market place.

A key Carlson property (above and opposite page, top) is the new Radisson Plaza Hotel and Plaza VII office complex. The 36-story, $108 million addition to the Minneapolis skyline opened in 1987.

Carlson Investment Advisory Group. Front row, from left: Marilyn Carlson Nelson, Curt Carlson, Barbara Carlson Gage and Edwin C. "Skip" Gage. Top row, from left: Dean Riesen, president, Carlson Real Estate Company; John Nagel, vice president, finance; Darrel M. Hamann, vice president, tax; and Rodney M. Wilson, president, Carlson Investment Group. Total assets are $400 million.

Real Estate Investments

"Riches have wings," wrote Francis Bacon in 1625. "Sometimes they must be sent flying to bring in more." Curt Carlson had the vision to send his capital winging even while Gold Bond trading stamps were his main business. In the 1950s, and continuing in the 1960s, Carlson looked to real estate investment, buying suburban farmland west of Minneapolis which would eventually become the site of his current and future world headquarters.

Today, Carlson Companies operates its own Investment Group under President Rodney M. Wilson, who manages a diversified investment portfolio with its primary emphasis in real estate. Carlson's real estate holdings include some 60 properties with total assets of $400 million. Real estate investments range from luxury hotels and restaurants to office buildings, office/warehouses, shopping centers and residential housing throughout North America. Non-real estate investments include securities, mortgage notes, oil and gas ventures, and equipment leasing.

"Carlson Investment Group," says Rod Wilson, "includes all the investment activities or businesses where income is derived from assets. Simply put, we own assets that people will pay money for — in rentals, royalties or interest. This part of Carlson Companies is asset-driven rather than sales-driven."

Carlson's biggest real estate investment is Plaza VII, a $108 million, 36-story hotel and office complex on the site of the original Radisson Hotel in the heart of Minneapolis. Carlson also has a joint-venture interest in Carlson Center, a $650 million mixed-use development on 325 acres of prime wooded land near two of the busiest highways in the Minneapolis—St. Paul metro area. A ten-year plan, the realization of Carlson's vision from the 1950s, will be executed by Texas-based Trammell Crow Company, the nation's largest developer of commercial real estate. Opening in 1989 will be Carlson Companies' new world headquarters.

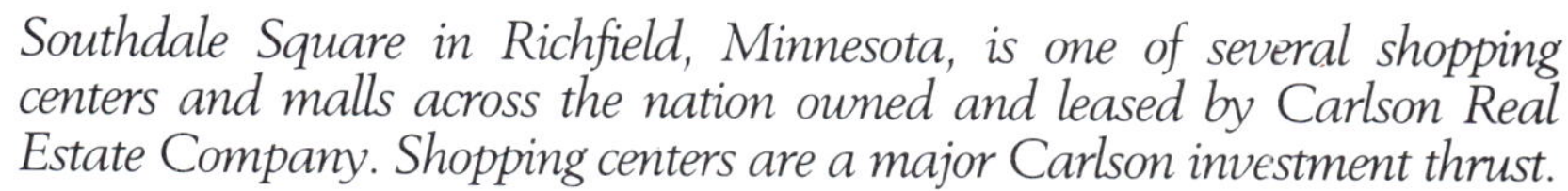

Plymouth Oaks Park is one of several innovative showroom/warehouse units which Carlson Investment Group rents to companies. "When you go into real estate," says Curt Carlson, "you need 'patient' money."

Southdale Square in Richfield, Minnesota, is one of several shopping centers and malls across the nation owned and leased by Carlson Real Estate Company. Shopping centers are a major Carlson investment thrust.

Letha and Charles Carlson, the parents of Curt Carlson, pictured on the day they became engaged to be married. The mother, who would give birth to four sons and a daughter, was a strong family figure and managed the home with a firm and loving hand. Like Curt, the father was a salesman and during hard times supported the family in the wholesale grocery business, and later, owned a neighborhood food store.

Family

Last year, *Fortune* magazine published a cover article called "Should You Leave It All to the Children?" It opened with an elegant color photograph, spread across two pages, of Curt Carlson, his wife, Arleen, and their two daughters and their husbands. Under the outdoor family portrait, the caption quoted Carlson: "How do we keep our money from destroying our kids?"

It is a question that has agonized most wealthy families. Curt Carlson doesn't claim to have all the answers but he firmly believes that traditional values — the work ethic, striving for excellence, close family ties and solid religious faith — are the most sure avenues leading to a life of achievement, worth to society and a personal sense of fulfillment.

Carlson is devoted to his family and most of his leisure time orbits around his wife, daughters Marilyn and Barbara and their husbands, seven grandchildren and a multitude of nieces, nephews, and cousins. Several times a year, scores of them congregate at Carlson's Minnesuing Acres Conference Center (the "Lodge") in northwestern Wisconsin. It's a special brand of Swedish family reunion.

Curt and the immediate family attend church services every Sunday and often have brunch together afterwards. Most Swedish immigrants were Lutherans but the Carlsons became Methodists partly because the mother worked in the home of a Methodist minister. Letha Carlson lived to see son Curt become a centimillionaire and her only concern was that he should slow down a little, enjoy life and spend more time with the family.

"She was right," says Curt, "and I've always tried to be home on Sundays even when we were working killer-hours and six-day weeks to build this business. Wouldn't it be all for nothing," he says pensively, "if you're making money but losing your family."

The Minnesota entrepreneur grows emotional when he thinks of "Mom" Carlson and the sacrifices she made when he was growing up as one of five children in a Minneapolis neighborhood. It is a tribute to his own parents, and especially to Letha Carlson, that he works so devotedly to maintain family solidarity. And as one philosopher said, there's a link between harmony in the home and peace among nations.

Curtis LeRoy Carlson at age six. Born in Minneapolis to Swedish-American parents on July 9, 1914, he was the third of five children. Hard work, self reliance, family and religion were the Carlson credo.

Curt Carlson never takes work home and he always treasured and protected his time with the family, even in the early days of building his business. Holiday events have delighted daughters Marilyn and Barbara since childhood days. Right, Curt carves the Thanksgiving turkey.

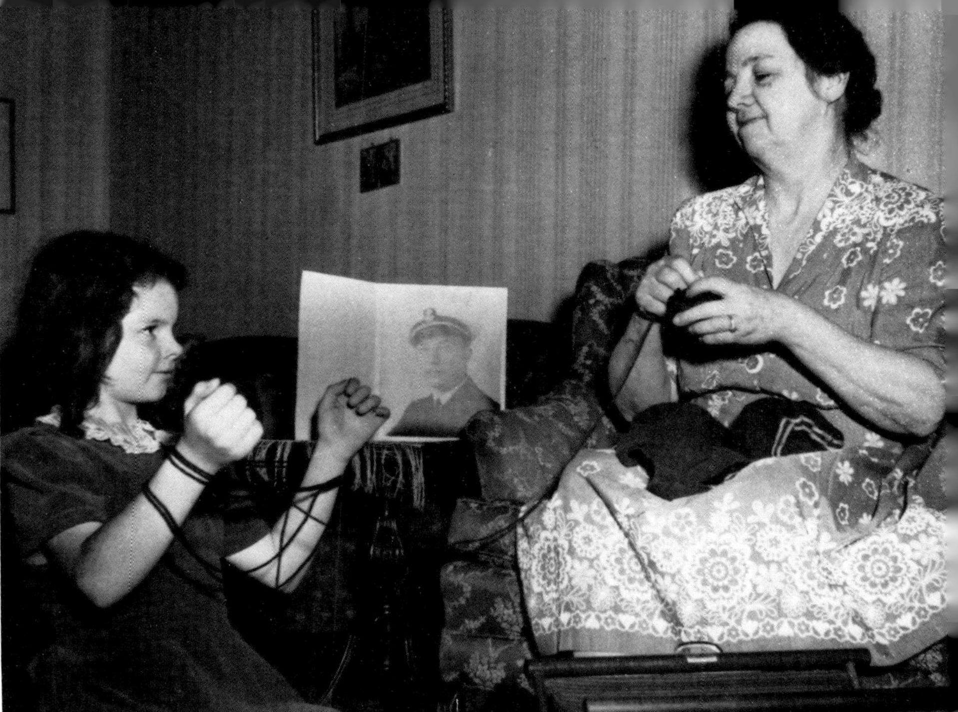

As a youngster (above), Marilyn Carlson enjoyed helping grandmother Letha with her knitting and other chores. She is the older of the two Carlson daughters and active in the affairs of the family business.

Fond of horses and outdoor life, Carlson was captain of the Shriners horseman parade unit in Minneapolis and named this favorite steed "Captain." At 74, Curt still enjoys riding in the Wisconsin woods.

Proud grandparents, Curt and Arleen "coo" with four-month-old Diana. Their first grandchild became an advertising executive with a major New York firm before marrying in 1987. She has plans to pursue an MBA degree at Northwestern University in Evanston, Illinois.

"Surrey with the fringe on top" carries Curt and Arleen, up front with their golden retriever. Passengers include Barbara Carlson Gage, Dr. Glen and Marilyn Carlson Nelson with Diana, their first-born.

The "Lodge" at Minnesuing Acres has become a traditional gathering spot for the extended Carlson family and Curt organizes talent shows for entertainment, with every member participating. Here, a few years ago, he pretends that grand-nephew Jamie, now a Protestant clergyman, could use a bit more practice before showtime.

Minnesuing Acres Conference Center in Wisconsin's north woods is mainly a business retreat but occasionally a family leisure haven for the Carlsons. Curt and Arleen enjoy the clean air, picturesque lakes, sunwashed days and starlit nights. Situated in the center of Lake Minnesuing is an island. Carlson's father owned a cottage on the island and Curt spent summers there as a youngster. After the birth of his daughter Marilyn, Curt bought nearby property so his family could appreciate the pleasure of spending summer weekends amid woods and lakes.

Sunday services at Hennepin Avenue United Methodist Church in Minneapolis is a family tradition. Curt and Arleen with the grandchildren: Wendy, Geoff, Curtis, Ricky, Diana, Christie, Juliet and Scott.

Ambitious like his grandfather Curt, young Curtis Nelson (below) is working as a hotel trainee in San Francisco and developing plans to make his own mark in the thriving hospitality business.

The Carlson home is located on Lake Minnetonka in a wooded section west of Minneapolis. Top left: Arleen enjoys her rose garden and a view overlooking azure waters. Inside, Curt and Arleen ascend a spiral staircase from an inside pool area to reach an entryway decorated with marble columns, classical statuary and Parisian wall murals.

Married in September, 1987, to Marius Muresanu, Diana Nelson wore a Swedish wedding crown used in the parish church of Curt Carlson's ancestors for some 300 years.

The **Curt-C** is an 85-foot luxury yacht that Carlson Companies operates primarily for business purposes. The elegant vessel sails to Caribbean and Gulf of Mexico ports out of Florida. There's sun, balmy breezes, high seas relaxation and fine food, wine and personal service.

In 1984, Carlson's family surprised him with a 70th birthday party "at sea" on Minnesota's St. Croix river. Wife Arleen notes that her "captain" of industry is not an easy man to surprise. The happy-birthday cruise included entertainment by Cliff Brunzell (pictured with violin, background on bow) who was musical conductor, leader and one of the original Golden Strings violinists at the original Radisson Hotel.

Each July 4th and Christmas holiday, some 60 members of the Carlson family assemble at Minnesuing Acres Conference Center "Lodge" in northwestern Wisconsin for food, games and the fun Curt brings to family gatherings.

Left, Curt hoists the flag to show that the owner is on the premises and ready to welcome guests.

Wendy Nelson (daughter of Marilyn) enjoys her own special relationship with grandfather Curt. The entire Carlson family, including nephews, nieces and cousins, look forward to holiday celebrations at the Lodge.

Minnesuing Acres Conference Center, used by businesses all over the nation, opened in 1961 in the pristine wilderness of Wisconsin. It features home cooking, rustic interiors, full recreational facilities and even a stocked trout pond. The Center is on Lake Minnesuing, an Indian word which means "island with water around."

Stairstepped by age (left), the four Carlson brothers and their sister are a close-knit family. From top: Kenneth, Aileen Carlson Miller, Curt, Dean and Warren.

Right: granddaughter Diana Nelson surprised the '86 summer family celebration at Minnesuing "Lodge" by posing as Lady Liberty in tribute to the Statue of Liberty bicentennial.

Below left: the Carlson family "Olympics," where pie-eating ranks as one of the most competitive — and laughable — events.

Below right: Curt reads Jimmie and Melissa Morford a classic fairy tale by Selma Lagerlöf, the famous Swedish author and Nobel Prize winner who was Curt's ancestral cousin. The youngsters all call Curt "Boppa."

The Edwin C. Gage family, festooning the traditional tree at Christmas-time. Father "Skip" and Mother Barbara are pictured with daughter Christie and sons Ricky, Scott and Geoffrey.

The Dr. Glen Nelson family, pictured right at the home of Curt and Arleen Carlson beside Lake Minnetonka west of Minneapolis. Dr. Glen and Marilyn are at left with their daughters Wendy, Diana, Juliet and son Curtis. Juliet (far right) died in a tragic auto accident in 1986.

twin cities
WOMAN ™
THE FORUM FOR MINNEAPOLIS-ST. PAUL WOMEN
$1.00   3 Sections   Volume 2/Number 3   March 1978
Did Father
Really Know Best?

The answer to the magazine-cover question (left) is "Yes," according to Carlson's daughters Barbara (left) and Marilyn. "Daddy's always been quite a workhorse," says Barbara, "but what you need to understand is that when he's with you, he's really there." Sister Marilyn agrees that her father is single-mindedly "focused" on family, business, faith and the Swedish heritage he shares with millions in the Midwest.

Joining the business in 1968, Edwin C. "Skip" Gage (far left) was named president and chief operating officer in 1984. At the installation banquet, Curt had grandchildren Scott, Christie and Ricky "crash" the formal event with signs and cheers. At right is Skip's wife, Barbara.

Roots

First and always, there is the land.

And the land is embraced, held fast, by roots. Roots not only of trees and wildflowers and crops, but also of the people. The plain, hard-working people who put down *their* roots — roots of building, marriage, bearing and rearing children, and burying their dead. Roots of agriculture to eat and survive and create commerce. Roots of long-forgotten memories that can be unearthed and read like runic inscriptions, helping to explain a man and his extraordinary success in the New World.

The roots of Curtis L. Carlson, ultra entrepreneur and the most successful Swedish-American, can be traced to the Swedish provinces of Värmland and Småland. Extensive research by Dr. Arne Linnarud (a cousin of Curt Carlson), has produced a rich repository of family lore. Linnarud has sketched a family tree whose limbs stretch to some of the most famous names in Swedish arts and letters, clerical families including a renowned bishop-poet, owners of ironworks and members of the top level of 18th and 19th century society.

But Carlson's closest kin were not rich landowners and barons of Sweden's lucrative ironpits. They were farmers mostly. Dr. Linnarud begins the story by linking a young girl with a young oak tree. "Let us imagine a scene in the Carlson annals," he writes. In 1854, a baby girl was born at a small homestead at

Curt Carlson's father was born in the Swedish province of Småland and emigrated with his parents to America in 1886. The family home no longer stands but it undoubtedly resembled this house of handhewn timbers and grass-sod roof which is the birthplace of Carl Linnaeus, the famous Swedish botanist who was also a product of rural Småland.

Svenstorp, near Rottneros, in the parish of Sunne, Värmland — a province in west central Sweden that is much nearer to Oslo than to Stockholm. She is Kristina Nilsdotter, the paternal grandmother of Curt Carlson. From the yard she could enjoy an enchanting view of Lake Fryken.

When the lake lay dark under heavy rain clouds and the north wind swept through the valley, it was time for Kristina to leave her outdoor games and help her mother, Kajsa, with the chores. The azure-blue water could be seen through the spruce and pine branches, imagines Linnarud, even after the first leaves of spring had thickened into heavy foliage. In winter, the smooth hillsides were perfect for gliding on the wooden skis that her father Nils (the great-grandfather of Carlson) had fashioned for her.

In the center of the yard there was a small oak tree. The oak is uncommon in these parts and no doubt Kristina and her brothers and sisters had been cautioned to treat it with care. Before she was 20, Kristina left the yard and the oak tree to marry Karl Adolf Bergström Karlsson, a man from Småland, 200 miles to the southeast.

In 1886, Kristina, her husband Karl Adolf, and their four young children pulled up their roots and emigrated to the United States. The oldest child was six, the youngest a babe in arms. A boy of three named Charles was to be the father of Curt Carlson, who today marvels at the strength and determination of his grandparents: "That to me shows true courage: To leave everything you have behind, to strike out for a new land with nothing but a bagful of hope."

Like thousands of other Swedish immigrants, they settled in Minnesota's "Moberg country." Vilhelm Moberg was the Swedish author whose powerful novel *The Immigrants* was made into motion pictures. The Karlssons farmed a plot near North Branch, 30 miles north of Minneapolis. Kristina, the girl who played near the oak tree in Värmland, would bear six more children before dying of "consumption," or tuberculosis, in her 40s.

Her son Charles would grow up, leave home to work in Minneapolis at age 19, and marry the daughter of other Swedish immigrants from Boyceville, Wisconsin. Her name was Letha Peterson and she would give birth to four sons and a daughter. The one in the middle would be Curtis LeRoy Carlson, who, nearly a century after his father left Sweden, would seek out the oak tree in Värmland. The house where Kristina lived is gone but the oak tree is still there. And Curt Carlson could almost see the spirited girl who would become his grandmother playing in that long-ago yard. She stops to rest against the rugged bark of the oak tree — a living link with the past, its strong roots still embracing the ancient and ever-lasting land.

The people of Värmland and Småland differ in character. And just as it is interesting to compare the traits of a stolid New Englander with a drawling storyteller of the U.S. deep South, it is instructive to examine the characteristics of Carlson's ancestors in the Swedish provinces.

Värmlanders," explains Dr. Linnarud, "have an easy way about them; in fact, they may seem almost undisciplined. Many people consider Värmlanders pleasant with their talkative ways and their inability to take things seriously. They are considered to be good craftsmen but unable to hold onto money. They recoil from the idea of hurting others, which can sometimes lead to complications. The phrase 'We'll see' is the same as a definite 'No' spoken mildly. The non-Värmlander fails to understand this distinction but imagines that 'Perhaps' is the same as a promise. When nothing comes of it, they speak of 'unreliable Värmlanders'.''

None of this remotely hints of the character of Curt Carlson. Thus, Dr. Linnarud finds it "totally incredible" that a businessman of Carlson's calibre could have his roots in Värmland. He writes: "No Värmlander — with the exception of L.M. Ericsson, creator of the Swedish telephone company — has ever been responsible for a successful venture of any size. The Värmlander is not a natural businessman or, anyway, not a successful one." So look elsewhere for genetic explanations of Carlson's success.

Look to Småland, the other side of the Carlson coin. The Smålander is tough, not fond of flowery language, conscientious in the extreme, good at saving, patient and uncomplaining with his lot. A well-known saying goes: "Put a Smålander on a rock in the sea and he will make crops grow on it and soon have both a cow and goat." Apparently, the combination of Värmland and Småland is a highly successful one. Exhibit A: Curt Carlson.

Carlson is a good listener and a gifted storyteller. So was his talented cousin, Selma Lagerlöf (1858-1940). Trained as a schoolmistress, she created novels rooted in Swedish legend and saga, and her stories were powerful in their mood and imagery. In 1909, she became the first Swedish writer and the first woman to win the Nobel Prize for Literature. It says much of her character that with the prize money she bought back the family house at Mårbacka which had been sold after her father's death. In 1914, Lagerlöf became the first woman elected to the Swedish Academy.

The rustic charm of a field in Småland embraces wild vegetation and primitive fences. Rocks, grubbed from the earth, make room for farming.

A zealous pacifist and feminist, she interceded through the Swedish royal family in 1940 to save the German-Jewish poet Nelly Sachs, a future Nobel Prize laureate (1966), from a Nazi concentration camp.

Selma Lagerlöf's first major work (1891) was the two-volume *Gösta Berlings Saga*, a chronicle of life in her native Värmland during the prosperous era of iron founders and small manors. When the novel became a motion picture years later, it launched the Hollywood career of Swedish actress Greta Garbo.

Nils Holgersson was one of Selma Lagerlöf's most popular characters and she wrote two books about the boy who was transformed into an elf. Nils flew between his adventures on the back of a tame goose, an entrancing image that has been commemorated on a Swedish postage stamp. These stories were used extensively in Swedish schools, being especially useful as geography readers for children, and were translated into 50 languages.

Elegance among wildwood, Nottebäck Church sits in Småland province near Växjö, where Esaias Tegnér — noted poet and a relative of Curt Carlson — was Lutheran bishop from 1824—46. Carlson's father attended services here and many relatives lie in the graveyard.

Sentimental about Sweden and fascinated by his expansive family tree, Carlson — the American cousin — arranges a bouquet for his oldest living relative. She is 93-year-old Elin Holmquist, who lives in a home for the elderly in the parish of Gräsmark.

What might be regarded as a forerunner to the Radisson hotel chain, this farmhouse at Lövåsen near Sunne, Sweden, was operated as an inn for about 250 years by relatives of Curt Carlson. Marita Tagesson and her young daughter display a family "heirloom" — the sign removed from the old inn in 1924 when lodging was no longer offered. The Swedish word "Gästgiveri" advertises a combination of inn and restaurant.

Another creative ancestor of Carlson was the brilliant poet and cleric Esaias Tegnér (1782-1846). His family was poor, his father dying and leaving no money when Tegnér was nine. But the boy was such a talented student that he received schooling and graduated from the University of Lund, later being appointed a professor of Greek there. In 1824 he became the Lutheran bishop of Växjö and retained the position all his life. Tegnér's poetic achievements have been widely translated and he made famous the Swedish word *Levnadslust* — "joy of life." More than perhaps any other in the Swedish-English dictionary, it captures the affable poise, the joyful attitude and the smiling intelligence of the Swedish personality mirrored in Curt Carlson.

Another author of note in the Carlson genealogy is Anna-Maria Lenngren (1754-1817). A published poet by age 18, she was educated by her father, a lecturer at the University of Uppsala. She married the co-founder and editor of the influential *Stockholmsposten* and contributed anonymously to the newspaper. Her poetry — mostly classical satires and pastoral idyls — is remembered for its elegance of style, purity of diction and remarkable gaiety.

A tragic but immensely gifted poet from the same family tree, also a son of Värmland, was Gustaf Fröding (1860-1911). First a journalist in Karlstad, he was beset by emotional illness most of his adult life. But he was a master of humorous verse and, as one critic puts it, "His popularity as a poet was enhanced by the appeal of his personality, which remained essentially kind, noble and upright despite the tragedy of his life."

In modern times, Curt Carlson had common interests — and common ancestry, in a Finnish lineage — with Tage Erlander, the late Swedish Prime Minister. Erlander and Carlson never met but the political leader was passionately interested in Löv-

Curt and Arleen Carlson and two of their grandchildren — Wendy Nelson and Scott Gage — visit Gräsmark church in Sweden's Värmland province near Sunne. At center is Elin Holmquist, at 93, Curt's oldest living relative. In back: Arne and Moira Linnarud; he has done genealogical research on Carlson's ancestors back to the 1600s.

Left: Photos taken 90 years apart of the home of Carlson's maternal grandmother, Kristina, in Värmland province; she played under this tree as a young girl before marrying and emigrating to the U.S.

åsen, near Sunne, the home of his (and Carlson's) forefathers, and in the history of the farm with the oak tree. In 1983, a television program focused on Erlander's ancestry and included a visit to the village.

The farm and inn at Lövåsen in Värmland province reveal some of the deepest roots of Carlson's family tree — a dozen generations starting with Påvel Olofsson Suhoinen about 1594 and his family's emigration from the Finnish lake district.

There today, one finds a neatly-restored farmhouse which various Carlson cousins operated as an inn for almost two and one-half centuries, about 1680 until 1925. Researcher Linnarud calls it a "17th century Radisson Hotel." The present owner, Lars Tagesson, is the 11th generation of the Suhoinen family and the Lövåsen pioneers. His son Christopher, born in 1985, is the 12th.

The few roads in Värmland in the 1680s were hardly passable by coach and most travelers went horseback. Inns in the rugged area were few and far between; indeed, one map from the 1680s shows not a single lodging in the entire Fryken Valley community. One of 11 planned inns mentioned in a court document of the period was at Lövåsen, the home of the Suhoinen family and a link to Curt Carlson.
An example of the service at the "Lövåsen Radisson" and charges are found on a price list from 1781:
- 1 meal, better quality, 6 skilling; poorer quality, 4 skilling.
- 1 bed for night, better quality, 3 skilling, poorer quality, 2 skilling.
- 1 mug of ale, 1 skilling and 4 runstycken.
- 1 candle, lasting 2 hours, 4 runstycken.
- 1 bundle of hay (8.5 kilos), 4 skilling.

The skilling would be only a few cents in modern currency and the runstycken only one-twelfth of that. Travel, like life itself, was cheap.

This forerunner of the Radisson chain was operated by three of Påvel Olofsson's seven sons without the benefit of bell captains, credit cards and computer reservations. In winter, guests were crowded together in one room and in summer, less insulated quarters and outbuildings were used. Horses were needed for farming and forestry and the innkeeper's duty to provide horses for travelers in winter was far more cumbersome than directing them to a rent-a-car clerk. Descendants of Daniel Olofsson, one of the original sons, have continued working at the farm home for some 330 years — which leads us back to Lars Tagesson.

In 1984, Curt Carlson and his wife, Arleen, together with their two youngest grandchildren, visited the Värmland village that Carlson's Swedish forefather had cut out of the wilderness.

Lars Tagesson and his wife, Marita, received them with warm hospitality — like long-lost American cousins — and proudly guided them around the farmhouse, barn and grounds.

In nostalgic awe, they saw the farm museum assembled by Lars' father, Tage Olsson; he had collected everyday tools and antiques from bygone days, many of them used in the innkeeper's trade. Carlson was intrigued by a couple of planks, which were probably placed between two doors of the original old inn. They bear this inscription:

Here I eat my bread
here I worship my God
Bless all who go out
and in here. The year of 1812.

Selma Lagerlöf wrote wondrous stories. And the most engaging and enduring character of all was a boy named Nils who turned into an elf and traveled all around Sweden on the back of a tame goose. In this old sketch, Selma receives the 1909 Nobel Prize for Literature from Gustaf V, King of Sweden and great grandfather of the present king.

Authoress Lagerlöf and others in the Carlson genealogy — most of them writers, journalists and poets — have been honored on Swedish postage stamps: Gustaf Fröding, Anna-Maria Lenngren and Esaias Tegnér.

Swedes who get to know Curt Carlson on his visits to the homeland have been impressed by his pleasant manner and his well-rounded store of knowledge even of areas far removed from his profession, and naturally by his far-ranging business achievements.

During the zenith of Swedish immigration to the United States, immigrants sometimes criticized the old country fairly severely, berating Sweden's social ills and lack of opportunity. During this period, the phrase was coined that "To be a good American, one must be a good Swede." In honoring his heritage, Curt Carlson is both a good American and a good Swede.

The Kinship Monument, a gift of Värmland province, commemorates the bonds between Sweden and America. Located at Rottneros, Curt Carlson's ancestral home, it was dedicated in 1953 by dignitaries of the United States, Sweden, Finland and five neighboring nations.

To trace the path of his parents to American shores, past the beckoning Statue of Liberty, and the chaotic gateway at Ellis Island, we must return to northern Europe and examine the conditions which made leaving Scandinavia not only appealing but an almost essential option for some two million of the poorer farming and labor classes trapped in a socio-economic vise.

Curt Carlson's father — and the parents-to-be of his mother — were among the more than one million Swedes who emigrated to the New World between 1860 and 1910. They came for opportunity, the hope for a better life, escape from hard times, and sometimes, relief from religious and political intolerance.

In 19th century Scandinavia, most people were tied to the land. And the land was harsh — most of it mountainous, forested, and infertile, with a short and fragile growing season. As Sweden's population increased, and only the eldest son could inherit the father's farm, the other children had reason to feel pessimistic. Meanwhile, lumberjacks and carpenters were losing jobs as iron replaced wood in the shipbuilding industry, and a restrictive guild structure stymied artisans and craftsmen.

In America, young men were told, you get land for $1.25 per acre and "whether native born or foreign, one is free to do with it whatever one pleases." In teeming American cities, there were jobs paying five times the wages one received in Europe. Young women were lured by the hope of a servant's job — who knows, even marriage. The scene was set: it took only a series of poor crops in the late 1860s to trigger the large-scale population movement. And all but the poorest could afford the $15 ship's fare to freedom's shores to forge a new destiny.

Rich in color and history, this painting of Swedish immigrants sailing into New York harbor past the Statue of Liberty hangs in a museum at Växjö, Sweden. The father and grandparents of Curt Carlson were among one million Swedes who came to America between 1860 and 1910 in search of a better life, freedom and opportunity. They made the journey in 1886, the same year the famous statue was finally dedicated.

The year was 1886, the same year that Bartholdi's "Liberty Enlightening the World" was rising on Bedloe's Island in New York harbor. France's famous gift to the United States would become a spiritual symbol for the incoming waves of freedom-seeking immigrants.

Karl and Kristina Nilsdotter Karlsson — Curt Carlson's grandparents — left Sweden's Småland province and turned their hopes and dreams toward the distant prairies of Minnesota. Their ancient Viking forebears had visited New World shores centuries before. But these bold new explorers came to transplant their roots, to stay.

Philanthropy

Curt Carlson believes that business success carries the responsibility of being a corporate good citizen and neighbor. And he personally subscribes to Methodist founder John Wesley's dictum: "Earn all you can. Save all you can. Give all you can."

Carlson Companies reflects the board chairman's commitment to humanitarian causes and improving the quality of life in all its dimensions. Through the Curtis L. Carlson Foundation, philanthropy is part of corporate philosophy and it is expressed not only through charitable contributions and grants — especially in support of education — but also through public service to non-profit organizations and agencies.

Years ago, Carlson was one of the founders of the Minnesota Five Percent Club, a prominent group of Minnesota-based business leaders who donated five percent of earnings to public service causes. The group, now known as the "Minnesota Keystone Awards," has been nationally recognized for its progressive approach to community responsibility. The concept has been studied, admired and imitated by major corporations and cities.

In 1986, Carlson gave a personal gift of $25 million to his alma mater, the University of Minnesota. It was the largest single gift ever presented a public university and the kick-off for the "Minnesota Campaign" under Carlson's dynamic leadership. The fundraising drive hit $305 million plus in 2½ years to help the University achieve academic status as one of the top five public institutions of higher learning.

Accompanied by cap-and-gowned faculty, Carlson prepares to receive an Honorary Doctor of Business Administration degree from Nathaniel College in Antrim, New Hampshire. It is one of several honorary degrees conferred on the entrepreneur/advocate of higher education.

Raising their fists in victory salute on the occasion of reaching the half-way mark of a drive to raise $300 million for the University of Minnesota are Dr. Ken Keller, left, university president, and Curt Carlson, chairman of the drive. Called "Commitment to Focus," the campaign aims to move the University of Minnesota into academic ranking among the top five public universities in America, and make it a fulcrum for economic development and stability for Minnesota. In 1986, Carlson made a personal gift of $25 million to spark the drive.

As a tribute to his late friend, Carlson also funded the $1 million "Carlson Lecture Series" at the University's Hubert H. Humphrey Institute of Public Affairs. The series annually brings to the campus both national and international leaders to address the critical political and social issues of our time.

On the international scene, Curt Carlson — honoring his Scandinavian heritage — has been one of the most active, involved and generous supporters of Swedish-American affairs.

In their own communities, thousands of Carlson Companies employees contribute to civic betterment with their donations, involvement in community life, and concern for the public good. It's good business to be a good neighbor. The 50th anniversary logo/motto of Carlson Companies says it all: "Private Companies with a Public Conscience."

Since the 1960s Carlson has contributed over $30 million to worthy causes. Among them: donations to the arts, including the world-famous Minnesota Orchestra, the Shriners' Hospital for Crippled Children and the Swedish Academy of Science to advance work in space at that nation's Canary Islands site.

For this generosity, *Town & Country* magazine selected Carlson as their philanthropist of the year (1987—88) by giving him the "Generous American Award." The magazine calls Curt "a visionary with a different tactic. A selfmade man legendary for turning his ideas into profit, he has long applied the precepts of business to charitable giving… inspired the new philosophy of corporate giving."

In October, 1986, the University of Minnesota's School of Management officially became the Curtis L. Carlson School of Management. A 1937 graduate in economics, Carlson attended at reasonable tuition cost during the Depression, an opportunity he has generously repaid.

Curt and Arleen Carlson-enjoy sports and are ardent "Gopher" boosters of University of Minnesota athletic teams and other special events.

Campus sweethearts, they met in a political science class in the mid-1930s and celebrate their 50th wedding anniversary in 1988.

Thomas "Tip" O'Neill, the former Speaker of the U.S. House of Representatives, hugs Marilyn Carlson Nelson. He came to the University of Minnesota as a "Distinguished Carlson Lecturer" in the series made possible by Carlson's major contribution to address public issues.

Carlson supports youth programs. Pictured at an annual Boys' and Girls' Clubs dinner in 1980: the late Bert Gamble, board chairman of Gambles hardware store chain; the late Hubert H. Humphrey and his wife, Muriel; entertainer Bob Hope; and Curt Carlson.

Curt Carlson chats with Rudy Boschwitz, U.S. senator from Minnesota. Like Carlson, Boschwitz is an entrepreneur; he started Plywood Minnesota Inc. and is a staunch supporter of business and industrial development to provide more jobs for Minnesota.

Carlson and the late Marcus Wallenberg, Swedish banker and industrialist, were honored at the first annual Swedish Council of America Awards dinner in 1981. Curt, proud of his Swedish roots and heritage, was named "Swedish-American of the Year."

Curt and Arleen with entertainer Cab Calloway of "Hi de ho" fame. The Carlsons enjoy a wide circle of friends among actors, musicians, sports figures and other celebrities who once stayed and performed at the original Radisson Hotel in Minneapolis.

Carlson chats with Vice President George Bush, another "Distinguished Carlson Lecturer" at the University of Minnesota. Other Carlson Lecturers have included Barry Goldwater, German Chancellor Helmut Schmidt, Coretta Scott King, George Will and Alexander Haig.

Honoring his friend, Carlson led a $12 million drive to fund the Hubert H. Humphrey Institute of Public Affairs. From left: the late Vice President Humphrey, former U.S. Secretary of State Henry Kissinger, Carlson, and ex-Minnesota Governor Wendell Anderson.

Former U.S. President Jimmy Carter, who came as a "Distinguished Carlson Lecturer" to the University of Minnesota, was greeted by Curt and Arleen. The $1 million lecture series, open free to students and the public, honors Curt's close friend, the late Hubert H. Humphrey.

Koinonia, a hospitality ministry of the Hennepin Avenue United Methodist Church where Curt Carlson and his family are active members, is a place where people gather to deepen their relationships with self, others, earth and God. The retreat and conference center can accommodate groups from 18 to 110 people of churches, family reunions and youth groups. Through rest, play and worship, groups such as clergy, educators and professional care-givers have a chance to get away for planning, meditation and renewal of spirit.

In memory of his mother, Letha Carlson, Curt gave land, this chapel and a library to Koinonia, an ecumenical church retreat and conference center situated on 90 rolling, wooded acres near Annandale, Minnesota, on Lake Sylvia, an hour's drive from the Twin Cities.

Philip Habib, former U. S. ambassador, was a "Distinguished Carlson Lecturer" at the University of Minnesota series made possible by Carlson Companies and the Hubert H. Humphrey Institute of Public Affairs. Curt Carlson gave $1 million for the lecture series.

In 1982, King Carl XVI Gustaf presented Curt Carlson with the prestigious Linnéan Medal, awarded by the Royal Swedish Academy of Sciences. The Swedish-American businessman has also received the Royal Order of the North Star Commander. Carlson's father emigrated from Sweden in 1886 to Minnesota with his family. His mother's family were also Swedish immigrants, settling in Wisconsin. Below: Carlson the American entrepreneur meets Ingvar Carlsson the Swedish Prime Minister in his first official visit to the White House in Washington.

Curt Carlson is U.S. honorary chairman of "New Sweden — '88," a national celebration for both the U.S. and Sweden marking colonization 350 years ago of what is now Delaware. His Majesty Carl XVI Gustaf and Queen Silvia, whom the Carlsons have hosted previously, visited 15 U.S. cities in 1988. Above, the Minnesota entrepreneur pauses on a Stockholm bridge with a riverside view of the King's palace.

Future

The future belongs to those who prepare for it, seize its opportunities and shape it to their vision. Carlson Companies is guided by a strategy for the future, bringing to the world marketplace of the 1980s and 1990s a network of synergistic companies poised to meet the challenges of the 21st century. Meantime, Carlson's new headquarters is rising and global markets, including China, are being penetrated.

Scanning that horizon, Curt Carlson states that "A successful company must continually analyze and anticipate society's needs, develop ideas to meet those needs, and carry those ideas to fruition in the marketplace." Placing Carlson Companies in this competitive cosmos, Skip Gage adds with conviction: "We are one company with a unified mission. We want to be the best in every business we are in. We are customer driven. Simply stated, our business is service."

Travel is burgeoning. The hospitality industry — hotels and restaurants — is booming. In marketing, motivation and sales promotion, Gage believes the biggest growth will come in moving motivation techniques from sales into the workplace of the service industries. Transplanting quality control and incentive systems from the manufacturing plant into the office represents enormous opportunity, he believes.

Carlson Parkway is the main artery of the new $650 million, 325-acre Carlson Center to be developed in the late 1980s and 1990s. The "city within a city" development is 10 minutes drive west of Minneapolis straddling the suburban communities of Plymouth and Minnetonka. Carlson Companies' new world headquarters will open here in 1989. Carlson Center is being developed and leased by the Trammell Crow Company, the largest developer of commercial real estate in the nation.

After half a century of solid growth, the company that Curt Carlson built went over the top in 1987 to become a $4 billion private corporation. One of Carlson's secrets has been to find, train, motivate, reward and retain good people — from the senior executive ranks down through the rank-and-file.

"Money is *not* the name of the game," Carlson tells his colleagues. "The idea is to have some fun making a living. You keep score with the money as each goal is achieved. The key to success is believing in yourself and being able to surround yourself with good people."

Growth through entrepreneurship has long been the hallmark of Curt Carlson and the network of companies he has created. In his lifetime, entrepreneurs have become American folk heroes. President Ronald Reagan has said, "The greatest innovations for new jobs, technologies and economic vigor come from this small but growing circle of heroes — American entrepreneurs, the men and women of faith, intellect and daring who take great risks to invest in and invent our future."

Time, products, services and customers change. But within the Carlson Companies the entrepreneurial spirit of the founder and still-captain lives and thrives. Whatever the future holds, the men and women of Carlson Companies are prepared for the 21st century. When he decides to step down, this will be the legacy of Curtis LeRoy Carlson. One of a kind. A special breed. Curt Carlson: ultra entrepreneur.

Top Carlson Companies executives focus on "Growth Thru Innovation" at Minnesuing Acres Conference Center in northwestern Wisconsin, January 17–20, 1988. Carlson Companies and other leading corporations regularly use Minnesuing Acres for business meetings and seminars.

Breaking ground for new Carlson Companies world headquarters (from left): Stewart Stender, Trammell Crow Company, developers of Carlson Center; Plymouth Deputy Mayor David Crain; Kirt Woodhouse, Trammell Crow Company; Edwin C. "Skip" Gage; U. S. Congressman Bill Frenzel; Curt Carlson; U. S. Senator Rudy Boschwitz; Minnetonka Mayor Larry Donlin; Ann Richardson and Rodney Wilson, Carlson Companies.

Ice sculpture model of new Carlson Companies world headquarters was carved by Radisson Hotel South chefs and unveiled by Curt Carlson. The founder stated his belief that the new headquarters and Carlson Center development "will give Carlson Companies a running start to meet the challenges of the 21st century."

Carlson Center, a massive business and industrial park, is being developed by Trammell Crow Company, the nation's largest real estate developer. It will rise on what was Minnesota farmland outside Minneapolis when entrepreneur Curt Carlson, looking to the future, acquired the property in the 1950s and 1960s.

Twenty-first century architecture will characterize the new world headquarters of Carlson Companies. The twin towers are served by a common lobby and overlook a manmade lake. Most of Carlson's manifold corporate activities will be centered here upon its opening in 1989.

"Skip" Gage on the Future

The year 2001 is not far away. Our company will be much more international in the future because consumers in other nations, with their growing economies, will be demanding the kind of service businesses we offer. I believe this will be true in all our major business categories — hospitality, travel, and marketing.

Many of our individual businesses will, of course, undergo substantial changes by the year 2001. I can envision Ask Mr. Foster transactions taking place between our travel agents and a consumer utilizing in-home computers and video screens; the client would be able to look at specific destinations, hotels and hotel rooms, and tourist attractions.

In our major business categories of hospitality, travel and marketing, we will be a more significant and dominant factor in the future. As we continue to focus on our key business areas, I believe we will gain increasing market share and hold a stronger position in the marketplace. We won't stand still as major opportunities come along and we are confident Carlson Companies has the ability to be a major force in business categories we can barely imagine today. To put it another way, the 21st century awaits…

Edwin C. "Skip" Gage

130

Carlson Cos.' Skip Gage and Curt Carlson

Curt and Skip: the team that built Carlson Companies

OVER THE years, the mythology of Curt Carlson has grown so pervasive that comparatively little attention has been paid to his business entity — its past, present and future. Curt himself is such an entertaining personality — Horatio Alger, super salesman, showman, desk-pounder, 3 a.m. phone-caller, risk-taker extraordinaire — that it's easy to

It was with obvious fondness that Curt recounted the story he's told so many times — about how he started his company at the end of the Depression with a $55 loan and against all advice to the contrary.

Carlson's trading stamp company, the Gold Bond Stamp Co., had an unusual characteristic: two distinct tiers of customers. There

Curt Carlson on the Future

As we approach and cross the threshold of the 21st century, I see the Carlson Companies remaining, for the most part, private. It will be entirely controlled by my immediate family and their children. I feel that the advantages in remaining private still outweigh public ownership, particularly when you see so many firms and their stockholders haggling destructively for control of companies.

I see us emerging as strong leaders in the hospitality and travel industries — probably the most influential pacesetters in these areas.

I envision our motivation, marketing and incentive business growing, increasing its leadership as the largest and most successful in the world. I predict our revenues will hit $15—20 billion or more by the year 2001. We will continue our pattern of internal growth plus selective acquisitions. And our acquisitions will continue to focus on companies which are synergistic to the present industries in which we are already operating.

And when Carlson Companies celebrates its 100th anniversary in the year 2038, this proud founder will be there in spirit.

Curt Carlson

Future generations will benefit from educational opportunities made possible by Curt Carlson's support of the University of Minnesota. Thanks to his personal contributions — including a gift of $25 million — and his spearheading of the $300 million Minnesota Campaign, the university is destined to become one of top five public institutions of higher learning in the nation. Carlson was a 1937 economics graduate.

Carlson Companies already has affiliate-company operations spanning the globe but the future holds promise of further development of international markets in hotels, restaurants, travel, marketing, motivation and sales promotion. Curt Carlson and "Skip" Gage are leading one of America's most successful private corporations to the ongoing fulfillment of the company motto, "Growing and Going Globally."

132

This fantasy Radisson hotel (No. 1,000?) and resort city reflects the brilliant imagination of Robert T. McCall, official artist of NASA, the U.S. space agency. Of this conception, McCall says: "Since anything man can imagine seems possible, perhaps the time will come when he can control the effects of gravity. Then this incredible hotel-resort sus-pended in the sky could become a reality. This vision of the future would be largely self-sufficient with its own transportation center, recreation facilities and all the amenities of a great resort. Such a 'floating city' could cruise the world for the best possible climate, environment and events calendar." In Carlson Companies' next 50 years, who knows?

Important Dates in History of
CARLSON COMPANIES, INC.

1938

Gold Bond Stamp Company founded and developed by Curtis L. Carlson.

1938–1952

Gold Bond trading stamps slowly worked their way into the Minneapolis marketplace, then regionally.

1953

Gold Bond trading stamps introduced into one of the nation's largest food chains — Super Valu food stores — the first large supermarket chain in the nation to use trading stamps. Almost overnight, Gold Bond trading stamps became a household word for Americans.

1955

Gold Bond trading stamps introduced into Canada. Today, Gold Bond is the largest trading stamp company in Canada.

Company moved into own building at 1629 Hennepin in downtown Minneapolis.

1959–1960–1961

Joint venture acquisition of 1,000 acres for home office and Minneapolis Industrial Park (MIP).

1960

Formed jointly with Grand Union — Performance Incentives Company.

Acquired 50% interest in Radisson Downtown Hotel.

1961

Opened Minnesuing Acres Training Facility — "the Lodge" — on the shores of Lake Minnesuing, Wisconsin.

Started advertising agency — Adams, Martin and Nelson.

1962

Gold Bond Stamp Company headquarters opened in Plymouth, Minnesota.

Contract Service Associates officially formed and begun.

Acquired remaining interest in Radisson Hotel in downtown Minneapolis, Minnesota.

1962–1963

Bought out majority of partners in Minneapolis Industrial Park.

1963

Company name changed to Premium Service Corporation (PSC).

Launched Gift Stars Coupons on various grocery and grooming aid products.

1964

Acquired Red Scissors Coupons (Premium Associates).

1965

Gold Bond trading stamps introduced in Hawaii.

Acquired Aloha Stamp Company.

Acquired Holden Stamp Company.

Acquired Security Stamp Company.

Acquired 51% interest in Canning Co., Trinidad, West Indies.

Gold Bond trading stamps introduced in Caribbean nation of Trinidad-Tobago, West Indies.

Conceived and built Superior Fiber Products, Superior, Wisconsin; a joint venture with Superior and Duluth businessmen.

1966

Built Pacific International Building, (4 stories) Honolulu, Hawaii. (6-story addition in 1968)

Introduced Gold Star and Gift Bond trading stamps in Japan.

1967

Launched, nationally, Gift Stars coupons on packs of Old Gold cigarettes. Gift Stars coupons redeemable with Gold Bond stamps at Gold Bond Gift Centers.

Acquired Leuthold Travel Service, Inc.

1968

Gold Bond Stamp Company, in a joint venture with Mitsubishi, the Japanese industrial giant, introduced Gold Star and Gift Bond trading stamps throughout Japan.

Acquired Robinson Seidel — Twin Cities incentive company — part of which was a travel agency.

Acquired remaining 50% of Performance Incentives Company.

Number of trading stamps issued nationally by all companies reached peak year.

Acquired Frontier Stamp Company. (Included Family Park Shopping Center, Flintwood Shopping Center and Park Central Shopping Center — all in Lubbock, Texas).

Acquired majority interest in May Brothers Company, food wholesalers, Minneapolis, Minnesota.

Started Direct Mail Division.

Acquired Gold Crown Stamp Company.

Edwin C. "Skip" Gage joined the company.

1969

Launched, nationally, LMC Coupons on packs of Chesterfield cigarettes. LMC Coupons was a joint venture between Carlson Companies and Liggett and Myers. LMC Coupons redeemable with Gold Bond Stamps at Gold Bond Gift Centers.

Built and opened Radisson Mart, downtown Minneapolis, Minnesota.

1970

Acquired Radisson Denver Hotel, Denver, Colorado.

Purchased 25% interest and assumed management of new Radisson Duluth Hotel, Duluth, Minnesota.

Opened Haberdashery Restaurant-Pub in the Radisson Downtown Hotel, Minneapolis, Minnesota.

Built and opened new Radisson South Hotel, Bloomington, Minnesota.

1971

Gold Bond purchased Melior Stamp Company in Belgium.

Acquired John Plain/Pick-A-Gift/John Plain Incentives — a direct mail and incentive company.

1972

Acquired all but small percent of outstanding stock in May Brothers Company, Minneapolis, Minnesota.

Established Carlson Properties, Inc. — real estate development.

Acquired Ardan Wholesale, Inc., Des Moines, Iowa — catalog showrooms.

1973
Purchased Security Life Building, Denver, Colorado.

Company changed name to Carlson Companies, Inc.

Opened Haberdashery Restaurant-Pub at 7 Corners in Minneapolis, Minnesota.

1974
Purchased Radisson Inn Atlanta, Atlanta, Georgia.

Opened Haberdashery Restaurant-Pub in downtown St. Paul, Minnesota.

Acquired majority interest in Superior Fiber Products, Superior, Wisconsin.

Assumed management of Radisson Muehlebach Hotel, Kansas City, Missouri.

Built Radisson Inn Plymouth, Plymouth, Minnesota, with MTK Japan as minority partner in hotel and majority partner in Japanese restaurants.

1975
Acquired Gold Strike Stamp Company, Salt Lake City, Utah.

Assumed management of new Radisson Inn Grand Portage, Grand Portage, Minnesota.

Acquired TGI Friday's — Restaurants.

Built and purchased minority interest in Grenelefe — a Radisson Resort, Cypress Gardens, Florida.

1976
Acquired Gold Star Stamp Company, Montreal, Canada.

Acquired K-Promotions, Inc., Milwaukee, Wisconsin.

Acquired complete ownership of MIP.

Purchased 50% interest and assumed management of Radisson St. Paul, St. Paul, Minnesota.

Purchased Northern Federal Building in downtown St. Paul, Minnesota.

Assumed management of Radisson Arrowwood Inn & Resort, Alexandria, Minnesota.

Built, purchased 25% interest and assumed management of Radisson Burlington Hotel, Burlington, Vermont.

Acquired over 50 percent interest in Indian Wells Company — natural gas and petroleum company — Kearney, Missouri.

Acquired A. Weisman Company, Minneapolis, Minnesota.

1977
Purchased 20% interest in and assumed management of new Radisson Plaza Charlotte, Charlotte, North Carolina.

Acquired Maple Plain Company, Maple Plain, Minnesota.

Acquired Jason/Empire, Inc., Overland Park, Kansas.

Purchased Eastridge Mall, Gastonia, North Carolina.

Acquired Country Kitchen International, Inc., Minneapolis, Minnesota.

Launched Cash Dividend Coupon plan nationally.

Achieved $ 1 billion in annual revenues.

1978
Acquired Naum Bros., Rochester, New York — catalog showrooms.

Purchased and took over management of new Radisson Scottsdale Resort & Racquet Club, Scottsdale, Arizona.

Acquired NSI Marketing, Canada.

Assumed management of Radisson Chicago Hotel, Chicago, Illinois.

Purchased 20% interest in NCNB Building, Charlotte, North Carolina.

Assumed management of new Radisson Ferncroft Hotel & Country Club, Danvers, Massachusetts.

Acquired WaSko Gold Products, Corp., New York, New York.

Purchased Southern States Cooperative Corporate Building, Richmond, Virginia.

Acquired Omega Sports, Maryland Heights, Missouri.

1979
Acquired Trek Travel, Canada.

Assumed management of Northstar Inn, Minneapolis, Minnesota.

Purchased Shiman Bros.—Colonial, Inc., New York, New York — jewelry manufacturer.

Purchased 25% interest in and assumed management of new Radisson Wilmington Hotel, Wilmington, Delaware.

Started and purchased 50% joint venture interest in Curtis Homes, Minneapolis, Minnesota.

Acquired Incentive Services, Inc., Chicago, Illinois.

Purchased 30% interest in and assumed management of new Radisson Plaza Nashville, Nashville, Tennessee.

Formed North American Financial Corporation (NAFCO) — leasing company.

Acquired Performax Systems International, Minneapolis, Minnesota.

Acquired Sports Films & Talents, Inc., Minneapolis, Minnesota.

Acquired First Travel Corporation, Van Nuys, California — included Colony Hotels, Firstours, Ask Mr. Foster travel agencies and Transportation Consultants, International.

1980
Premium Group name changed to Carlson Marketing Group, Inc.

Established Hotel and Resort Group to include Radisson Hotels, Inns and Resorts and Colony Hotels and Resorts.

Assumed management of Ramada Inn, Rochester, Minnesota, under National Hotel Corp.

Assumed management of new Radisson Inn Saginaw, Saginaw, Michigan.

Purchased 18% interest in and assumed management of new Radisson La Crosse Hotel, La Crosse, Wisconsin.

Built with 50% interest in and assumed management of new Radisson Plaza St. Paul, St. Paul, Minnesota.

Acquired Spotts International, New Brighton, Minnesota.

Acquired Integro (Inter Personal Growth Systems, Inc.) Minneapolis, Minnesota.

Acquired Communication Arts, Minneapolis, Minnesota.

1981

Purchased 20% interest in and assumed management of new Radisson St. Louis Hotel, St. Louis, Missouri.

Acquired E. F. MacDonald Motivation Company, Dayton, Ohio.

Acquired Henniker's, Salem, Virginia, from Stuart McGuire Company.

1982

Assumed management of new Radisson Plaza Hotel, Raleigh, North Carolina.

Purchased 10% interest in and assumed management of new Radisson Oasis, Cairo, Egypt.

Assumed management of new Radisson Inn and Yacht Club, Barker's Island, Superior, Wisconsin.

Assumed management of new hotel, The Lincoln - A Radisson Hotel, Dallas, Texas.

Achieved $2 billion in annual revenues.

1983

Acquired Saproma (incentive motivation and marketing company), Cologne, Germany.

Acquired P. Lawson Travel, Ltd., Toronto, Ontario, Canada.

Acquired Creative Merchandising and Publishing, Minnetonka, Minnesota.

Assumed management of new resort, Minaki Lodge - A Radisson Resort & Conference Centre, Minaki, Ontario, Canada.

Purchased 10.5% interest and assumed management of new hotel, Radisson Hotel High Point, High Point, North Carolina.

TGI Friday's — Going public, 25% or 4.5 million shares — sold out first day. (December 8, 1983)

1984

Acquired Dolginow's of Missouri.

Purchased 9% interest and assumed management of new Radisson Hotel Lynchburg, Lynchburg, Virginia.

Acquired Cartan Tours, Inc., Rolling Meadows, Illinois.

Acquired Valley Travel, Phoenix, Arizona.

Purchased 20% interest and assumed management of new Radisson Mart Plaza Hotel, Miami, Florida.

Assumed management of new Radisson Plaza Hotel Indianapolis, Indianapolis, Indiana.

Assumed management of new Radisson Hotel Metrodome, Minneapolis, Minnesota.

Assumed management of new Radisson Inn Maingate, Kissimmee (Orlando), Florida.

Assumed management of new Radisson Hotel Centennial, Mesa, Arizona.

Acquired GTU Inc., (Group Travel Unlimited, Inc.) Alexandria, Virginia.

Radisson Hotel Corporation launches franchising program.

1985

Assumed management of new Radisson University Hotel, Minneapolis, Minnesota.

Purchased 25% interest and assumed management of new Radisson Mark Plaza Hotel, Alexandria Virginia.

Assumed management of new Radisson Hotel Charlottesville, Charlottesville, Virginia.

Assumed management of new Radisson Plaza Hotel Orlando, Orlando, Florida.

Assumed management with small equity in new Radisson Hotel Fargo, Fargo, North Dakota.

Radisson Hotel Corporation signed international partnership agreement with Mövenpick Hotels International.

Radisson Hotel Corporation entered an international partnership agreement with Hotels Paraiso.

Radisson Hotel Corporation signed an agreement whereby the 1,000-room Hotel Concorde La Fayette, Paris, France, became a Radisson-affiliated hotel.

Achieved $3 billion in annual revenues.

1986

Assumed management of new Radisson Hotel at Park Plaza, Oshkosh, Wisconsin.

Acquired Don Travel Service New York and Don Travel Westchester.

Assumed management of new Radisson Plaza Hotel, Austin, Texas.

Radisson Hotel Corporation entered an international partnership agreement with SAS International Hotels.

Carlson Hospitality Group announced plans for Country Hospitality Inns — a new national limited-service lodging chain.

1987

Opened Radisson Plaza Hotel Minneapolis/ Plaza VII Office Tower.

Broke ground for Carlson Companies' new World Headquarters at Carlson Center.

Radisson Hotel Corporation signed an international partnership agreement with Park Lane Hotels International.

Radisson Hotel Corporation signed an international partnership agreement with Commonwealth Hospitality Inc. of Canada.

Achieved $4 billion in annual revenues.

1988

Carlson officials set goal of $9 billion in revenues in 1992.

Carlson Companies World Headquarters building completed.

1989

Carlson Companies scheduled to move most of its major operations to new World Headquarters at Carlson Center.

Royal Order of the North Star Commander,
by H. M. Carl XVI Gustaf, King of Sweden, 1976

Awards & Honors

Swede of the Year, Svenskarnas Dag, 1966

Outstanding Achievement Award,
University of Minnesota, 1967

WCCO Radio
"Good Neighbor" Award, 1971

DeMolay Legion of Honor Degree, 1972

Honorary Doctor of Business Administration,
Nathaniel Hawthorne College, Antrim, New Hampshire, 1976

Minnesotan of the Year,
Minnesota Broadcasters Association, 1976

Minnesota Business *Hall of Fame* (Charter Member), 1976

National Distinguished Merit Citation
by the National Conference of Christians and Jews, Inc., 1977

Golden Plate Award
by American Academy of Achievement, 1977

Capital City Award
by St. Paul Area Chamber of Commerce, 1977

Great American Award
by International B'nai B'rith Foundation, 1978

Horatio Alger Award, 1978

University of Minnesota *Regents' Award,*
(University's Highest Award) 1979

Distinguished Service to Minnesota Award, Minneapolis Kiwanis Club, 1980

Harvard Business School Club of Minnesota, Honored Company Award, 1980

Swedish-American of the Year, Stockholm, Sweden, 1981

Executive of the Year, *Corporate Report Minnesota magazine, 1981*

Linnean Medal, Royal Swedish Academy of Sciences,
presented by H. M. Carl XVI Gustaf, King of Sweden, 1982

National Jewish Hospital/National Asthma Center Humanitarian Award, 1982

"Motivator of the Year" Award, National Premium Sales Executives (NPSE), 1984

Viking Baron Award, The American Swedish Cultural Foundation, 1984
(first American to receive this award)

Distinguished Community Service Award by the Anti-Defamation League of B'nai B'rith, 1985

Honorary Doctor of Humane Letters Degree, New Hampshire College, Manchester, New Hampshire, 1985

Honorary Doctor of Humane Letters Degree, Augustana College, Rock Island, Illinois, 1985

Silver Plate Award, Lodging Hospitality magazine, 1986

University of Minnesota School of Management renamed the "Curtis L. Carlson School of Management," 1986

Ellis Island Medal of Honor, Statue of Liberty-Ellis Island Foundation, New York, 1986

Twin Citian of the Year, Twin Cities magazine, 1987.

Thirty-Third Degree (honorary), Ancient and Accepted Scottish Rite of Freemasonry, 1987.

Generous American Award to one of the country's outstanding philanthropists, *Town & Country* magazine, 1987.

When this man says he gave at the office, he gave at the office.

Here's the inside story (and more) about this year's most Generous American,
plus several hundred runners-up…then we paint some colorful stories about Crayolas,
Carefree, Arizona and people who drive four horses with one hand.
All in your December <u>Town & Country</u>.

Town & Country's annual Generous American Award goes to Curtis L. Carlson, founder of Gold Bond trading stamps and philanthropist extraordinaire.

Since 1959 he's been donating 5% of his company's federally taxable income (he's the sole stockholder so the decision and the money is *his*) to help solve community problems. So far, he's given 30 million dollars at the office. And he preaches what he practices. He barnstorms the country talking fellow executives into doing the same.

And there's still more about Carlson and a generous number of other Philanthropic Americans starting on page 173. They include a big bundle of Super Santas and just about everyone you've ever heard of in Minneapolis.

Is this the most statuesque gift list ever given?

Our list of Super Santas for 1987—people and foundations who've made major contributions to art, science, scholarships and the humanities—include donations of $750 million and down. It includes one extremely thoughtful gift from Iris and Gerald Cantor—58 Rodin sculptures to the Brooklyn Museum.

to know that if the world's supply of petroleum ever runs out, Crayola has developed a crayon made of something else. Whew!

If someone's going to drink champagne out of your slipper, make sure you have a pair that goes well with pink.

Our man in the kitchen, James Villas, positively bubbles with enthusiasm about the Champagne Rosés that are popping up from Lutece to Lasserre to the First Class sections of Air France flights. Warning! He's not talking about those domestic pink things that have assaulted the tongues of collegiate sports since the days of F. Scott and Zelda. He's talking about the Ultimate Champagne of France. It's a difficult wine to make (one slip and it can come out the color of a banana), so it's a costly wine to buy. Before you lug home a jeroboam or three, read Villas' red hot recommendations.

Plus generous helpings of other information.

Discover the Morgan Library in New York where you can come across Voltaire's briefcase, Goethe's pen and Robert Browning's hair…what was in

©*Arnold Newman.*

Generous American Award to one of the country's outstanding philanthropists, *Town & Country* magazine, 1987.

Another Carlson Companies Goal Achieved!

Curt Carlson and members of the Metropolitan Boys Choir.

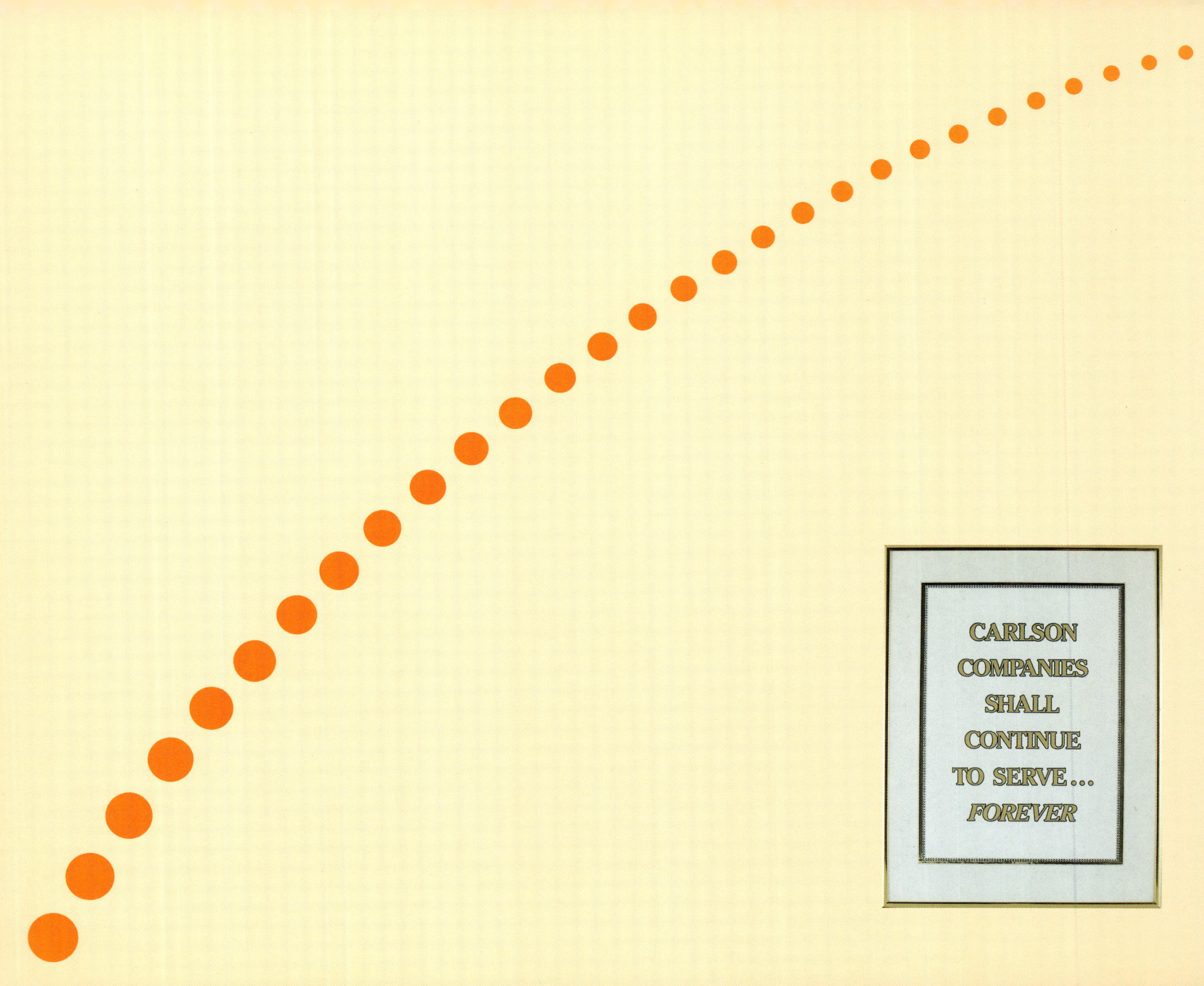

CARLSON
COMPANIES
SHALL
CONTINUE
TO SERVE...
FOREVER

Carlson Companies, Inc.
Carlson Center
701 Lakeshore Parkway
P.O. Box 41827
Minneapolis, Minnesota 55441
USA

612-540-5000

Telex 29 0996
FAX 612-540-5665
Cable Address CARLINTER

©	Curtis L. Carlson
Producer	Karl W. Gullers
Text	Willmon L. White
Special Advisers and Research	Tom Jardine and Tona Erickson
Photography	Dwight Miller, Betty Engle LeVin, Karl W. Gullers, Tom Jardine, Tom Polski, Larry Roepke, Mike Kuller, Peter Gullers, Hasse Persson
Printer	Tryckcentra AB, Västerås, Sweden 1988
Publisher	Gullers Pictorial Inc., Phoenix, AZ
ISBN	0-941250-01-6

Library of Congress Catalog Card Number 88-80059
Main entry under title: Curt Carlson — The Ultra Entrepreneur

Deep in the heart of Sweden's Småland province, the ancient farms, ponds and trees reflect a bucolic tranquility. Curt Carlson's father, born in this region, immigrated to Minnesota in 1886.